FAIRFAX HOUSE
YORK

An Illustrated History
and a Guide

PETER BROWN

YORK CIVIC TRUST

ABRIDGED FAIRFAX GENEALOGY

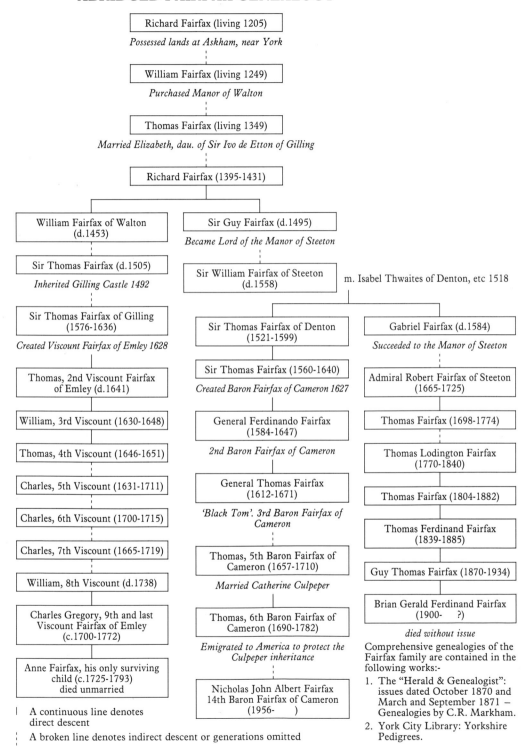

Richard Fairfax (living 1205)

Possessed lands at Askham, near York

William Fairfax (living 1249)

Purchased Manor of Walton

Thomas Fairfax (living 1349)

Married Elizabeth, dau. of Sir Ivo de Etton of Gilling

Richard Fairfax (1395-1431)

William Fairfax of Walton (d.1453)

Sir Guy Fairfax (d.1495)

Became Lord of the Manor of Steeton

Sir Thomas Fairfax (d.1505)

Inherited Gilling Castle 1492

Sir William Fairfax of Steeton (d.1558)   m. Isabel Thwaites of Denton, etc 1518

Sir Thomas Fairfax of Gilling (1576-1636)

Created Viscount Fairfax of Emley 1628

Sir Thomas Fairfax of Denton (1521-1599)

Gabriel Fairfax (d.1584)

Succeeded to the Manor of Steeton

Thomas, 2nd Viscount Fairfax of Emley (d.1641)

Sir Thomas Fairfax (1560-1640)

Created Baron Fairfax of Cameron 1627

Admiral Robert Fairfax of Steeton (1665-1725)

William, 3rd Viscount (1630-1648)

General Ferdinando Fairfax (1584-1647)

2nd Baron Fairfax of Cameron

Thomas Fairfax (1698-1774)

Thomas, 4th Viscount (1646-1651)

Thomas Lodington Fairfax (1770-1840)

Charles, 5th Viscount (1631-1711)

General Thomas Fairfax (1612-1671)

'Black Tom'. 3rd Baron Fairfax of Cameron

Thomas Fairfax (1804-1882)

Charles, 6th Viscount (1700-1715)

Charles, 7th Viscount (1665-1719)

Thomas, 5th Baron Fairfax of Cameron (1657-1710)

Married Catherine Culpeper

Thomas Ferdinand Fairfax (1839-1885)

Guy Thomas Fairfax (1870-1934)

William, 8th Viscount (d.1738)

Charles Gregory, 9th and last Viscount Fairfax of Emley (c.1700-1772)

Thomas, 6th Baron Fairfax of Cameron (1690-1782)

Emigrated to America to protect the Culpeper inheritance

Brian Gerald Ferdinand Fairfax (1900-   ?)

died without issue

Comprehensive genealogies of the Fairfax family are contained in the following works:-

1. The "Herald & Genealogist": issues dated October 1870 and March and September 1871 — Genealogies by C.R. Markham.

2. York City Library: Yorkshire Pedigrees.

Anne Fairfax, his only surviving child (c.1725-1793) died unmarried

Nicholas John Albert Fairfax 14th Baron Fairfax of Cameron (1956-   )

| A continuous line denotes direct descent

⋮ A broken line denotes indirect descent or generations omitted

Contents

Text and design by Peter Brown.
Chapter on The Owners by Gerry Webb.

Published by York Civic Trust,
Fairfax House, Castlegate, York YO1 1RN
Printed by Maxiprint, York, England.

ISBN: 0 948939 03 6 — A History and Guide
ISBN: 0 948939 04 4 — Tour of the House

Foreword

Fairfax House, far and away the best Georgian house in York, had been shamefully neglected and allowed to decay to a state of near collapse by its former owners and tenants.

The York Civic Trust and other organisations had campaigned for some forty years to preserve this important building but it was only in recent times that the opportunity for positive action presented itself through a series of remarkable coincidences.

In 1981 the Trust set about acquiring the house from the York City Council who had owned it for 15 years and who were ill disposed to putting it up for sale otherwise than by public auction.

At the same time Noel Terry (of chocolate fame) had recently died and his superb collection of Georgian furniture (said by Christie's to be the finest private collection of its period formed in the last 50 years and valued by them at over one million pounds) became available. He had always wanted it to be kept together in York and when his Trustees heard of the Civic Trust's efforts to buy Fairfax House they offered to give the whole collection to the Trust for display in Fairfax House if the City Council could thereby be persuaded to sell it privately. They were so persuaded and the whole of the £30,000 purchase price was provided by the National Heritage Memorial Fund, thus giving the house the hallmark of excellence. The Trust then set about the restoration and retained as its architect Francis F. Johnson, F.R.I.B.A. from Bridlington, a man of discernment, taste, and a passionate lover of the Georgian era with a great understanding of the architecture and furnishings of the period. The Civic Trust from its own resources and with the help of no less than £165,000 from the then Historic Buildings Council, raised the £750,000 necessary to restore the house to its former glory and it was opened by the Trust's Patron, H.R.H. The Duchess of Kent in October 1984.

As the visitor will see, the marriage of house and furniture has created a union of rare delight.

John Shannon
Chairman.

John Shannon, Esq., O.B.E., D.Univ.(York).

Francis F. Johnson, Esq., J.P., F.S.A., DIP.ARCH., F.R.I.B.A., D. LITT.

Introduction

The culmination of this remarkable project stands as a model of co-operation between government bodies, grant-making organisations and a small independent charitable Trust. Such rescue operations have little chance of success however without financial assistance from numerous sources and the York Civic Trust gratefully acknowledge the help of the National Heritage Memorial Fund, the Historic Buildings Council, the Trustees of the Noel G. Terry Charitable Trust, the Pilgrim Trust, the Leche Trust, the Bowes Morrell Trust, Wimpeys plc, Rowntree Mackintosh plc, and the trustees of the late S.H. Waller for contributing so generously to the costs of the restoration. Thanks are also due to the many friends who gave so freely to the setting up of the house, either by loaning items on display, or by being so forthcoming with their advice and help; to David Learmont, John Cornforth, the Bath Preservation Trust, the Bristol Art Gallery and the National Trust for their wise counsel and to the members of the House Committee of the York Civic Trust for steering the whole project to its successful conclusion.

When the house was first taken on, little was known about this branch of the Fairfax family but gradually over the years a clear picture has emerged that places the family in the context of the religious and political climate of the period and provides a rationale for the creation of this superb townhouse here in the middle of York.

A considerable amount of early work had been undertaken by H.G. Ramm, Eric Gee and Jim Williams of the Royal Commission on Historic Monuments and this, together with the studies of Hugh Aveling and R.B. Wragg forms the basis of our knowledge. Research undertaken in recent years, however, has helped to clarify many points and my gratitude is extended especially to Gerry Webb and Denise Priddey for their transcription and the indexing of the correspondence in the Newburgh MSS and also to David Alexander, Bernard Barr, Major D.R. Baxter, Geoffrey Beard, Peter Brears, Darrell Buttery, Pat Clegg, John Cornforth, Ruth Duthie, John Griffin, June Hargreaves, Ivan Hall, Francis Johnson, Elizabeth McGrath, Hugh Murray, Patrick Nuttgens, Barbara Peel, Dick Reid, Jacob Simon, Bill Taylor and Gerry Webb for contributing to our understanding with the fruits of their research.

My thanks are also due to Betty Frampton and Anne-Marie McDougall for their diligent work with the manuscript.

For ease of reference the guide is divided into logical sections and the separate section on the tour of the house pp.49-64 affords an opportunity to use illustrations that are not repeated in the body of the publication. As visitors go round they will see that the rooms have been presented in as sensible a manner as possible. Noel Terry in common with many true collectors found it difficult to resist the acquisition of a rare or unusual piece and it would be wrong to think that the furniture is arranged in an 18th century manner, for in order to do justice to the collection the great majority of the pieces have been put out on display. As a consequence our presentation creates a 20th century informality that in its own way gives Fairfax House much of its charm.

Peter Brown
Director

5

The front elevation with its red brick and stone dressings shows a symmetrical arrangement of 5 bays on 3 floors with a projecting centre section surmounted by a pediment and having a recreated oculus within the spandrel. A late Georgian building to the left was converted into a cinema entrance in 1920 and the facade has been remodelled to match in with Fairfax House.

The Building

The present house stands on a dominant site in Castlegate (or Castlehill), a road that was for centuries one of York's leading thoroughfares before the building of Clifford Street in 1880.

The area has been in continuous occupation since Roman times and Drake[1] records the discovery of a massive

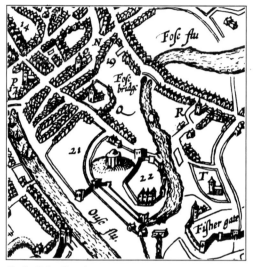

York, John Speed, c.1610.

Roman stone head found whilst excavating the foundations of a new house on a plot near to the Castle.

John Speed's map of York compiled in 1610 shows a series of half timbered buildings leading on down to the Castle entrance but they stop short of the entrance for a boundary stone standing some 25 yards outside the Castle gates marked the change from city to county jurisdiction. The site of the present building however enjoyed clear views across gardens to the rivers Ouse and Foss right up to the middle of the 19th century and it wasn't until a then Lord Mayor purchased and built on the un-developed portion of the Friary gardens

at the front, that the ambience of the area began to change. By the 1830s a huge prison wall had also appeared enclosing Clifford's Tower within the prison compound and the overbearing presence of this structure is clearly seen in Whittock's view of 1858.

Castlegate postern lane had as a consequence been laid waste and the reflective heat generated from the wall on a hot summer's day caused the area to be

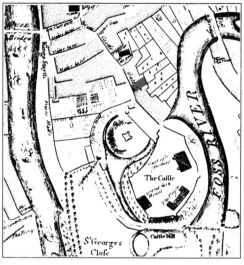

York, Peter Chassereau, c.1750.

nicknamed 'West Indies Way'. In 1879 some controversial road widening in the area[2] was to have a further detrimental effect on the setting, although this was alleviated somewhat by the creation of Clifford Street in 1880.

Fairfax House as we know it today gained its present name when the lawyer John Mayer negotiated the purchase of the house, grounds and parts of the adjoining property in August 1759 on behalf of the Honourable Anne Fairfax[3], only surviving child of Viscount Fairfax of Gilling Castle.

By arranging to hold the property in trust for the daughter through an intermediary, her father had neatly

York, South-east prospect, S. & N. Buck, c.1745.

avoided the problems of double land tax, a penalty levied on all Roman Catholic landowners who refused to renounce their faith. The deeds show that Mayer paid £600 for the house, about 10% more than the vendors had paid for it in 1749 and as land tax assessments for the period 1745-1773 had remained constant throughout[4], it is reasonable to assume that the body of the house had been constructed during the period 1740-1745. This helps to clear up several anomalies about the architecture of the façade and throws doubt on the suggestion that John Carr of York was responsible for the exterior.

Documentary evidence in the Newburgh papers[5] shows Carr to be heavily involved in the gutting out and the decoration of the interior during the period 1760-1762, but references to work on the shell of the house are scant. One notice in the York Courant[6] details the selling off of wainscotting from three rooms together with doors, door frames, oak beams and some old oak buffets and also refers to various sash windows of differing sizes. These sashes may have been removed at the front to make way for the unusual rusticated stonework seen on the ground floor windows and as this is very similar in style to stonework on the west front at Gilling Castle, it may be Carr's only work on the exterior.

Robert Davies,[7] writing on the Works of Carr states, ...'The most remarkable is the mansion in Castlegate, built for the last Viscount Fairfax of Gilling, which had originally a very imposing front elevation of red brick, with richly decorated stone dressings.'. . . . . During the Trust's recent restoration it was noted that most of the rusticated quoins and the oculus

8

had been hacked back flush with the brickwork at some stage probably due to the poor quality of the stone itself and that some of the stones have been incorrectly bedded. Excavations in the cellar also revealed that the house had no proper foundations and it was therefore necessary to raft and underpin to stabilise the structure before further work could proceed. It is unlikely that Carr, the son of a stonemason, would have countenanced such shoddy work.

Despite the misuse and abuse during the intervening years much of the original building had survived to the present time although consolidation and replacement was necessary on the rear elevation. In the roof space, open rainwater channels running through the void had taken the water to a central point at the rear of the house and this practice was discontinued in favour of external fall pipes.

Various principal beams bear testimony to work carried out in 1756, 1789 and 1811 and whilst these timbers were in remarkably good shape requiring very little work, the roof was stripped, retiled and given new lead valleys.

At ground floor level, a 19th century portico forming the main entrance to the

York, from the South-west, Nathaniel Whittock, 1858.

9

house was restored and underpinned, but regrettably during the 1879 road widening scheme an elegant set of wrought iron railings had been removed and these could not be replaced.

In 1919 the St. George's Hall Cinema Company had been granted permission to build a cinema to the side and at the back of the house and to convert the first floor rooms into a dancehall. It proved to be a remarkably insensitive conversion for such a fine house but in a curious way this contributed to its survival, keeping it out of the hands of the developers who in the 50s and 60s were to sweep away many fine examples of Georgian architecture in the city.

Fairfax House, c.1910.

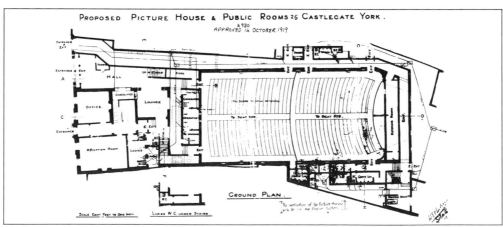

The Interior

Whilst uncertainty remains over Carr's influence on the exterior of the house, on the inside, his involvement is clear and total. The extensive bundle of Fairfax papers in the Newburgh MSS show Carr's influence not only in the major projects but also in some of the minor cosmetic works. The main section of papers directly related to the building programme of 1760-1762 are missing however, a curious fact that is held in common with many other country house archives where Carr was the architect, but sufficient evidence remains to confirm his considerable input and that of his favourite craftsmen.

In the entrance hall Carr's carefully contrived vista of arches coupled with the restrained ornamentation seen in the compartmented ceiling is very much in keeping with the Palladian concept of the crescendo where the degree of decoration reaches its peak in the principal rooms. Many of the decorative techniques employed, especially on the carved woodwork, are reminiscent of mouldings and patterns seen in other Carr houses, his clever use of a concave moulding on the doorcase architrave for example, accentuates its depth by a play of light and shade. In addition the acanthus leaf capitals on the pilasters, repeated on the inside of the main doorcase in Castlegate House across the road, are just two such devices taken from his accomplished repertoire of designs.

The great majority of Fairfax House's original decoration had thankfully survived, hidden beneath the cinema company's steel doors and heat-retaining canopy, but it was necessary to remove the Edwardian tiling in the entrance hall and return the floor to one of Elland stone and slate. Doors were repaired and re-hung, a repetition of the work carried out by William Grant in 1762 and the colour scheme reproduced, based on scrapings taken throughout the house.

Before and after views of the main entrance.

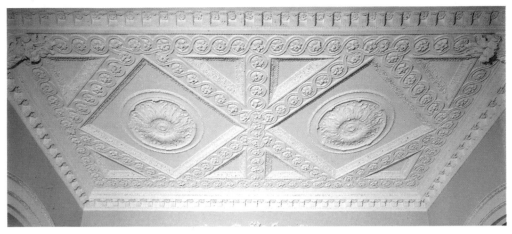

Compartmented ceiling with guilloche decoration.

In the staircase hall the decoration intensifies, utilising the popular guilloche pattern on the overdoor panels and diagonal banding of the ceiling that encloses a pair of Acanthus roundels.

Between the doorways and set high, is a draped stucco medallion of Roma Aeterna representing eternal Rome. She holds a winged Victory in her hand whilst below, at her feet, a goat and some sheep are in attendance. The goddess Roma was often used on the reverse of Roman coins and, as well as having a strong classic symbolism, it is likely that Viscount Fairfax saw this as a 'nod' in the direction of his religion. The only other known use of this allegorical subject in stucco was a similar medallion employed at Riverstown House in Ireland,[8] the home of Dr Jemmett Browne, Lord Bishop of Cork. C.P. Curran[9] reports that Raponi in his . . . . *'Recueil des Pierres Antiques Gravees,* Roma, 1786'. . . ., illustrates and interprets this representation, but he can find no satisfactory explanation for the attendant goat and sheep. It is possible however that in heraldic terms the goat may have had some significance to the Gilling branch of the Fairfax family.[10]

Roman Coin, c.200 A.D.

Stucco medallion representing Eternal Rome.

Library

One of the principal rooms on the ground floor and resplendent with its original fireplace, a duplicate of which can be seen at Lytham Hall in Lancashire.[11] There are contra-entry references in the family papers for payments of £15.5s.0d and £22.0s.0d to Mr. Cheere, but it is not clear whether these refer to the purchase of fireplaces or some other item intended for Gilling Castle or Fairfax House. As a young man Charles Gregory Fairfax spent most of his time in Europe. His father, the 8th Viscount, had been at some time a captain in the Austrian Imperial Army, drifting for over 15 years between garrison towns in Northern France, Lillie, Arras, Dunkirk and Douai, whilst Charles was sent to the Austrian monastery of Lambspring for his education. Apparently he did not share the same cosmopolitan interests and intellectualism of his relatives the Gascoigne family of Parlington[12], however he did develop an intense interest in current affairs, history and politics coupled of course with a great commitment to the Catholic faith. The sale of the library in 1793 created a great deal of local interest[13] and the five volumes of Chambers Encyclopedia of the Arts & Sciences acquired by his Chaplain Fr. Anselm Bolton, eventually found their way on to the shelves of the library at Ampleforth Abbey.

A portrait of John Carr in the library above the white and Siena marble fireplace.

After a terra-cotta bust by L.F. Roubiliac.

From an engraving by Faithorne.

From an engraving by Vertue after Kneller.

From a plaster bust by John Cheere.

The most obvious testament to the Viscount's literary aspirations can be seen in the four 'baso relievo' medallions garnished in oak leaves and set in panels on the stucco ceiling. Modelled from contemporary engravings and busts[14], they, more than anything written or visual, help explain the Viscount's feeling for home-bred piety, his great love of common sense and his finely tuned sense of humour. It would seem that much of his time was spent studying the various

virtually intact, protected in a paradoxical way by centuries of paint. Uses during the 20th century range from the Cinema Manager's office to storeroom to bicycle shed and during the Second World War, a coal rationing office, when the room had been divided in two by a partition wall. Thankfully the partition was made to fit around the fireplace. One of the most important decisions taken by Francis Johnson involved the removal of all the decorative

Library before.

Library after.

military campaigns of the day and he had been able to follow their progress on large cloth-backed maps purchased from his local bookseller John Hinxman. Other acquisitions were of a less serious nature and a purchase in 1761 of an engraving that illustrated a coronation wig, for example, showed more than a passing interest in fashion.

Restoration of the Library proved less of a problem than in some of the other rooms for the decorative detail was

woodwork from the house so that the thick layers of paint could be stripped off by tanking in baths of alkaline solution. Not only did this protect the carving during major building works but meant that the final finish was as crisp and as clean as it had been 220 years ago.

The cleaning of the ceilings however proved to be a major obstacle and just to remove the old paint from the stucco throughout the house cost in the region of £45,000.

Dining Room

Perhaps of greatest concern during the restoration was the state of the Dining room ceiling undermined in one corner by the leakage of a gentlemen's toilet directly above. It was fortunate that the combined strength of the stucco[15] plus the flexibility of the marsh reed to which it is fixed was sufficient to hold the sections in place and apart from repairing the cracks, the greatest effort went into the repair of the Doric cornicing. This series of inverted cones called guttae, forms part of the Doric order, one of Carr's favourite classical treatments and whilst one expects to see the use of this on an external cornice, as in the case of Castlegate House opposite, or more normally when enriching an entrance hall like those at Tabley, Lytham, Heath and Everingham, its use in a Dining room is quite unusual.

In contrast to this, the decorative scheme that the guttae enclose is typical of the period and accords very much with the sound principles of design that were expounded by Isaac Ware.[16]

The centre medallion shows a representation of Abundantia, holding an overflowing cornucopia of fruit and flowers in one hand whilst ears of corn are falling to the earth from the other. This design is taken from the illustrated works of Cesare Ripa,[17] a pattern book in great favour with the stuccoists of the day.

Secondary medallions of musical instruments and crossed wine glasses at her head and feet show suitable propriety for the setting and together with baskets of fruit and flowers, swagged garlands, scrolls, raffle leaves and ribbons, contribute to a decorative scheme of great virtuosity.

Some of the marsh reed showing through the damaged stucco.

The Dining room garnished with some of the famous 'Nanking Cargo'.

The polychrome fireplace is the only other example to survive the ravages of the cinema company and adds much to the general quality of the room. Set within its frieze is a replacement centre tablet that depicts Aesop's Fable of the Wolf and the Crane[18]. The Fairfaxes were considered modest entertainers in their day but occasionally they entertained some illustrious guests. Laurence Sterne dined here in 1767 although not as a friend[19], but as an intermediary for his patron Lord Fauconberg. It was a good excuse to let the wine flow and the cellar books of the day[20] reveal such quantities of port and wines being consumed that it is surprising that father and daughter were both able to live beyond 60 years of age.

Abundantia.
C. Ripa, 1645.

Crossed wine glasses smoking pipes and a punch ladle.

Wind instruments overlaid with the music of a Canon.

Enriched pilasters support an elaborate frieze and broken pediment.

Kitchen and Back Stairs

Food was an important part of Georgian life and the quantities this family consumed were as copious as their wines. Martha Brown, the Viscount's cook and the housekeeper Ann Pyatt, kept detailed records of payments and purchases[21] that have revealed a rich but surprisingly nutritious and balanced diet. An average week's purchase of fresh food included 112 lbs of meat, mutton and veal plus 12 checkins *(sic)*, 10 fouls *(sic)*, 2 geese, 2 rabbits, a quarter of lamb, some cod, turbart *(sic)*, lobster and a clutch of oysters. Eggs, milk and green vegetables were supplemented from the kitchen garden at the back[22] and Anne Baker maintained a regular supply of glazed Macaroons, Sugar Candy, Morrells and Truffles from her shop on Petergate. On special occasions, however, her husband William Baker was commissioned to create some spectacular centrepieces and charged the enormous sum of £15 15s. 0d for providing '5 large pyramids of wet and dry sweetmeats and all other things for 2 tables'[23] for a combined house warming and Viscount's birthday party for over 200 guests on April 14th, 1763. A skeleton staff of 11 servants had been brought over from Gilling for the winter season and their provisions were normally included in the day to day purchases, but this could only account for some of the beef, mutton and the chickens, leaving the remainder to be shared between Viscount Fairfax, his daughter Anne and the occasional guest.

In 1920, the two kitchens, servants' hall, larders and accommodation block were removed to make way for the cinema auditorium and the York Civic Trust have recreated an 18th century kitchen in what was probably the Back Parlour.

Smoak Jack spit (sic) and attendant ovens in the recreated Kitchen.

20

Back Stairs before
and after restoration.

The range, hotplate and its adjoining breadoven are by Green's of Halifax and are typical of those used in the latter part of the 18th century. The Smoak-Jack Spit *(sic)* mechanism, driven by a fan set within the chimney, is similar to the original system installed at Fairfax House. This was continually breaking down in the 1760s and Edward Hill the blacksmith was in regular attendance.

An 18th century oak food press or dole cupboard, a pine dresser with a contemporary plate rack and a kitchen table that converts into a settle, form the basis of the furnishings in this room and they are supplemented by a provincial longcase clock made by Joseph Hallifax of Barnsley. Time was very important to the cook and contemporary illustrations of late 18th century kitchens show similar provincial timepieces claiming pride of place.

Sugar was purchased by the loaf and the example on display is typical of the way sugar was supplied. Special scissors were used to break off pieces for cooking and in preserving, whilst spare loaves wrapped in blue sugar paper were hung from hooks in the ceiling to keep them out of the way of vermin.

Because the laundry room had been demolished, some of the laundry maids' equipment has crept into the kitchen on display, and both linen press and the two glass smoothing irons used to put shine back on Damask or linen tablecloths, give some idea of the labour intensive nature of this domestic work.

At the rear entrance of the house, elegant wrought iron stairs ascend to the top floor and in fact provided the only access to the guest bedrooms and long gallery on the 2nd floor. The cinema company had removed the bottom flight of stairs and these were reinstated using the pattern of the surviving balustrades.

The Leeds smith Maurice Tobin, perhaps the leading north country wrought iron and whitesmith of his day, had been commissioned to provide the originals and invoices also detail his involvement on the great staircase and on the railings at the front that had been swept away during the 1879 road widening scheme.

Tobin worked extensively for Carr throughout Yorkshire and at Harewood[24], he was working to Chippendale's designs for a stove and had supplied most of the iron grates and fire irons.

The Great Staircase

Maurice Tobin's greatest contribution at Fairfax House is seen in the balustrades on the principal staircase[25] a positive *tour de force* of ironwork that combines with the richly decorated woodwork and the subtle details of the plasterwork to create an architectural masterpiece of its age and a model example of a mid-18th century hall set in a townhouse on a restricted site[26]. The strong military theme of the ceiling centres around a representation of Military Architecture[27] and the elaboration of the coving with its warlike animals, precocious putti and weaponry both ancient and modern, demonstrates Fairfax's passionate interest in this subject and it may also by implication, be seen as a strong allegiance to King and country.

On the flanking walls, brackets support busts of Shakespear (*sic*) and Newton all set within a pair of highly accomplished stucco cartouches of swagged drapery and crossed palm leaves, a favourite motif of Joseph Cortese[28]. The other remarkable component of this accomplished staircase is the finely proportioned Venetian window with its solid veined marble columns[29] and the stone ballustrade below. The Corinthian capitals are based on the drawings of Palladio and are made of stucco built up around lead armatures, thus giving strength to the projections. These capitals support a fine stucco entablature and double arch that is reminiscent of the Venetian window in the South range of Wentworth Castle near Barnsley.

Fairfax had gone to great trouble to improve the view through this window and even purchased the small house next door from Mr. Hardisty so that by demolishing it, he would increase the light. The results were not satisfactory and he eventually asked John Carr to suggest improvements[30] but they were only cosmetic and may not have been carried out.

Much of the historiated decoration in the stucco ceiling is both allegorical and to some degree didactic, but some of the devices used would have little meaning to the Viscount's visitors unless they were scholars and followers of the Roman Catholic faith.

It was a rather risky thing to do but clearly the putti facing each other across the staircase are arranged in allegorical gesture and stance. On the south coving a plump little Amoretto holds a rococo pendant with pair of hearts in one hand and a flaming torch in the other that is intended to 'illuminate' the one true faith, whilst on the north coving the putto clutches some bolts of thunder and lightning, an allusion to the persuasive

The window had been bricked in and glazed over with opaque glass to hide the bricks.

power of eloquence, that he targets with his arrows on the ascending visitor. Less obvious but equally significant are the emblems and motifs applied to the various pennants. The two-headed eagles, St. Edward's crown and oak-leaf garlands for example are symbolic of the Holy Roman Empire[31] whilst the use of the Union Jack and the garlands of laurel leaf may allude to the Viscount's wish for reconciliation between the state and the Roman Catholic faith.

When the cinema company were using these stairs, the force of numbers had caused most of the steps to break where they join at the wall. Replacements were cast to the same pattern and some of the carved roses on the underside provided by Daniel Shillitoe's apprentices Matthew Ward and John Richardson[32], were reused in the construction. Each step was cantilevered in the same way but instead of the original oak wedges, expansion bolts were used to hold them in place.

The original busts of Newton and Shakespeare had been sold by the City Council in 1959 and these replacements are copies of those by Kneller in the National Portrait Gallery and by Fisher in the Minster Library respectively.

Tobin's wrought iron balusters ascend the restored cantilever staircase to the landing where four lavishly carved doorways (one is a dummy door) lead off to the bedrooms and into the Saloon.

The putto with its flaming torch and pendant cartouche filled with a pair of hearts is an allegorical statement by the Viscount and intended to symbolise the light of truth shining on the one 'true' religion.

Architettura Militare.

C. Ripa, Iconologia, Venice, 1645.

Ripa's *Iconologia* was written and illustrated for poets, painters and sculptors to aid them in their use of allegory. The first edition of 1593 was followed by ten others during the next two centuries and these volumes with over 400 illustrations and text, were to prove a great influence on art during this period.

George Richardson in his 1777 translation recommends 'an assiduous study of allegory, would thus render art singularly entertaining and intelligible to reason, taste and judgement. He (the artist) must present something more than is offered to the external eye and if he knows the right use of allegory . . . . to employ it as a transparent veil, which rather covers than conceals his thoughts'.

Anne's Bedroom

Used as a wash place during the days of the dancehall.

On 9th June 1762 and 21st June 1763, Samuel Carpenter received the sums of £9 0s 0d and £21 0s 0d on account of his painting at Fairfax House and these sums were to include a charge for the provision of mock India paper for the 'Misses Bedchamber' at 1/3d yard[33]. The quotes also make reference to some 201 feet of gilt border for this room although it is not clear whether this was supplied by the decorator or by the upholsterer George Reynoldson who provided most of the soft furnishings for the house and who also acted as general agent and factotum in the summer months when the family were at Gilling castle.

In more recent times during the occupancy of the cinema company, this room had been converted into a refreshments bar with access on the left to the dancehall. Windows had been blocked in and both chimneypiece and dado rail removed from the room.

The replacement fireplace with its elaborate Carron grate c.1770 came from Methley Hall near Wakefield, dem. 1960, another house where Carr was employed.

Above this hangs a portrait of Anne Fairfax in arcadian pose as a shepherdess, which originally came from Newburgh Priory[34].

Information that came to light some six months after the restoration was completed revealed that in 1765 the Reynoldson firm had invoiced the Viscount for providing a mahogany bedstead for Fairfax House with a gadrooned cornice and carved shell crest[35]. In the same invoice they also charged for 'taking the Crimson Damask bed curtains and vallens in pieces, carriage up and down to London and dying ditto' perhaps a reference to hangings taken from an old bedstead that had been freshened up and fitted to the new frame.

There had not been any four-poster beds in the Terry collection and this example designed by Francis Johnson in the Chippendale manner and made by Dick Reid of York, is hung with a moire silk. The tester has been fashioned from some carved pelmets supplied by the same George Reynoldson to John Grimston c.1755, for Kilnwick Hall, dem. 1950.

Anne Fairfax in arcadian pose as a shepherdess, surveys her restored bedroom.

Viscount's Bedroom

It is likely that when the Viscount used this room he had a clear view over the kitchen garden to the River Foss. In 1762 the walls had been hung with a green flock paper[36] and the Viscount's dressing room situated in the long narrow extension to the back, (demolished by the cinema company in 1920) had been decorated with blue flock. This daisy pattern paper, a design taken from the Temple Newsam Collection of historic papers[37] was felt more appropriate for a North facing room and the use of French chintz for the draped curtains and the hangings of the bed could well relate to the type of chintz that was supplied locally to the Viscount by the York firm of Tasker and Routh.

Despite the conversion of the room to a cloakroom during the days of the dancehall, the carved door surround together with some of the dado and skirting board had survived.

The pulvinated frieze above the door with its bold flourish of scrolls and interlinking foliage has, like other friezes in the house a delicate double flowering rose at its centre, perhaps based on varieties grown in the Viscount's garden[38], whilst the carved detail on the architrave has in this instance been mirrored in the enrichment of the skirting in an attempt to create a unified scheme. In the centre of the east wall a replacement fireplace, rescued from Methley Hall, restores the balance of this elevation and a doorway cut through on the South wall utilises an entrance formed in the 19th century and has been given a jib mechanism so that the rooms on either side can be returned to their original state. It is most unlikely that the Viscount would have subscribed to the idea of a connecting door between his

Used as a gentlemen's toilets in the days of the dancehall.

bedroom and the Drawing room. The furnishing is perhaps more in accord with what would be expected of a mid 18th century bedroom, although it is likely that the large press would have resided in the dressing room and be used to store the Viscount's suits and breeches on the shallow sliding trays. Tasker and Routh of York were also tailors to the Viscount and each year would make up two or three new suits for the Viscount in a variety of colours[39].

This branch of the Fairfax family were entitled to wear the livery colours of mulberry with silver trimmings but this combination was presumably not a rich enough mixture for the Viscount for most of his outfits were lavishly trimmed with gold lace and buttons.

Francis Johnson's design for the draped mahogany bed uses a French 'Persepolis' chintz and picks out some of the designs in the delicately painted tester.

The Drawing Room

In contrast to the restrained decoration of the bedrooms which were usually unseen by visitors, the principal rooms on the first floor were created in order to impress and enthrall.

Access to this the small Drawing Room could only be gained from the principal Saloon and was intended for the entertaining of close friends. Indeed the selection of Amicitia in the centre medallion of the ceiling as an allegory of Friendship, was highly appropriate[40]. John Carr had altered the internal dimensions of this room slightly to make use of a coffered coving, based presumably on ornaments taken from the Pantheon of Agrippa. The design draws the eye inwards to the centre and was a favoured technique he had employed to great effect on the great staircase ceiling at Lytham Hall. James Henderson the

C. Ripa, Iconologia, Venice, 1645.

York plasterer was paid 'Thirty Guineas in part for the Drawing Room ceiling', but it seems more likely that Joseph Cortese was employed by Henderson to do the fine modelling[41].

For many years this charming and beautifully scaled room formed part of a large L shaped ballroom into which both it and the adjoining saloon had been incorporated. During its days as a Dancing School the ceilings had been painted over with a dark red gloss paint and after some experiment it was decided to use gentle heat from a blow torch to soften the paint and scrape it off. The danger of spalling was reduced due to the presence of marble dust in the mix and the high level of strength and hardness of this stucco minimised any risk of blunting the finely modelled detail.

As in the bedroom the fireplace had been removed and this replacement of white statuary marble offset with green crossbanded Connemara is reputed to have come from Powerscourt House, Dublin. Replacement of the partition wall separating the two rooms required the carving of new overdoors and as no evidence remained of the detailing on this side, the designs of the doorcases in the bedrooms were used as the model. The extravagantly carved dado rail and skirting however had survived on some of the walls and replacement was based on these patterns. By tanking the original decorative woodwork in an alkaline solution it revealed work of great accomplishment. It also gave our present day craftsmen a clear design to work from and resulted in replacement carving every bit as good as that of 225 years ago.

The walls have been hung in a Green Cotton Damask[42] using an 'artichoke' pattern made popular in the late 17th and early 18th centuries and it seems unlikely that this room had been fitted out with curtains.

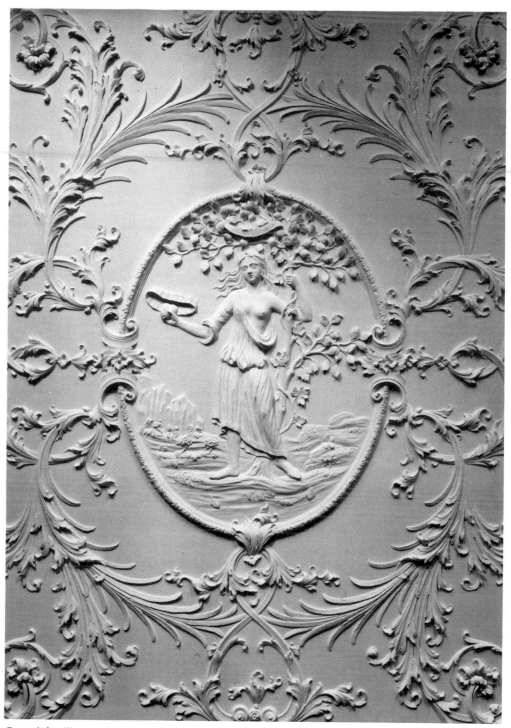

Cortese's familiar use of an interlacing pattern composed of curling stems interwoven with raffle leaves and narrower linear forms, provides an elegant setting for this interpretation of Friendship.

Bokhara carpets and walnut furniture complement the Damask covered walls.

The strength of Noel Terry's collection lies in the mid-18th century mahogany pieces but many of the earlier examples are displayed in the Drawing Room and the predominance of walnut blends well with the green walls and stone coloured woodwork. The painting over the fireplace is not part of the collection but bears the name John Tregeagle Esq. on the stretcher. It is of interest, however, because of the unusual manner in which the cravat is tied, a method referred to as a Steenkirk knot.

The name arises from the Battle of Steenkirk in Belgium in 1692 where the British under William III were defeated by the French led by Marshal Luxemburg. The French officers when preparing for battle, had to dress in a great hurry for the fray, twisting their cravats carelessly about their throats and passing the end through the buttonhole instead of tying a bow. It was to come into universal vogue throughout Europe[43] although the fashion had all but disappeared by 1725.

Bureau Bookcase, walnut, c.1700.

The Saloon

Perhaps the most accomplished of all the decorative schemes in the house, and most fashionable with its vigorous arabesque ceiling design incorporating a centre ellipse entwined by vines and linked to the swirling strapwork by some oak-leaf garlands. Medallions of crossed wind instruments indicate the room's intended use and the open manuscript of music above the fireplace has the popular 18th century ballad of Belinda and Amelia cut into the stucco. In the corners latticework baskets of fruit and flowers symbolise the seasons and illustrate, together with the arrangements in the Dining room ceiling, some unusual species of flower as well as the more expected varieties[44]. The whole ceiling is supported by a delicate cornice fringed with pairs of spouting lions, a device more associated with an exterior cornice rather than an interior one and below this a finely modelled frieze cavorts around the room and completes the sense of swirling movement.

The carved woodwork is of the same high standard and came from Daniel Shillitoe's workshops in Wakefield. Both door surrounds on the North elevation had survived the conversion into a dancehall but only one of the mahogany doors remained. Replacement of the East elevation and its decorative woodwork was undertaken by local craftsmen[45] and proved to be the same high standard as the work of 225 years ago. Nearly all of the remaining woodwork is original however and utilises many of Carr's favourite motifs and techniques.

In 1762 this principal room had been given a Crimson colour scheme but only four years later it was completely rehung in what was described as a 'sky mixt' damask by the York upholstery firm of Reynoldson[46].

Walls had been removed between the Drawing room and the Saloon to create the dancehall.

Restored to its original shape and hung with Damask once more.

J.F. Nollekens, A family in an interior, dated 1740. Acquired for the house with the aid of grants from the National Heritage Memorial Fund, National Art-Collections Fund (Rhododendron Trust), V. & A. Purchase Grant Fund, The Noel G. Terry Charitable Trust and Friends of Fairfax House.

A musical medallion above the fireplace.

The Universal Magazine of 1758.

The effect of this transformation must have been dramatic. Burnished Gold fillet was supplied costing almost as much per yard as the Damask and three pairs of lavishly fringed drapery curtains were hung to protect the room from the harsh effects of the sun. The Viscount's sofa, two armchairs and eight mahogany chairs were also upholstered in the same material and each one came back supplied with an individual blue and white check case cover.

The scale and intimacy of this room would have been ideal for the entertaining of small groups but in 1763, the Viscount wished to celebrate in style, not only his birthday but the completion of his new house and on April 19th of that year the York Courant reported: 'Last Thursday, being the Anniversary of the Birth of the Right Hon. Lord Viscount Fairfax, his Lordship gave an elegant Entertainment and a Ball to above 200 Gentlemen and Ladies at his magnificent new House on the Castlehill in this City, which is just finished.'

Two hundred and twenty years later despite the many vicissitudes, the house has been restored by the York Civic Trust to its former glory and furnished with what is considered to be one of the finest collections of mid-18th English furniture and clocks formed this century, re-creating what must now be considered as one of the finest Georgian townhouses in England.

Baskets of fruit and flowers contribute to the vigorous arabesque design of the Saloon ceiling.

The Restoration

The house had been subjected to appalling abuse and misuse during the last sixty years and a massive programme was necessary to save the building from imminent collapse.

The site had been bought from the cinema company in 1966 by the City Council who wished to protect it from indiscriminate development. They proposed various restorations and were finding it difficult to raise money for such a project out of public funds. One of the schemes floated was that of a Georgian museum and it was this concept that the York Civic Trust had had in mind.

By 1980, the Council was still unable to proceed and so under the inspired chairmanship of John Shannon, the Trust approached it with a view to buying the house and restoring it. With several important restorations to their credit and an excellent reputation already established, it was this credibility, combined with the acquisition of an outstanding collection of Georgian furniture for display in the house, which eventually persuaded the Council that this was the best option. A nominal sum of £30,000 was determined as the selling price with the clear knowledge that over £500,000 would be needed for restoration. The final figure of £750,000 reflects the nature of such projects where costs mount with every revaluation.

A restoration of this magnitude required an architect of great sensitivity to control and supervise each critical step and the Trust was most fortunate in securing the services of the eminent Yorkshire architect Francis Johnson and his partner Malcolm McKie. Francis Johnson, whose practice spans over 50 years, has often been described as a latter day John Carr. In his words: 'The survival

Charles Gurney working on the stone Oculus.

This 18th century door surround was used by the Trust on the side entrance of Fairfax House, beneath the great staircase window. It originally came from a house in Low Petergate, but was used latterly as a garden swing in Beckfield Lane, York.

Rear elevation before and after restoration.

of this house is a miracle. In all my career, which has involved literally dozens of country houses, never has there been such a challenge, nor a project which has so captured my imagination'.

Preliminary investigations revealed major problems with stability exacerbated by extensive piling operations nearby and there were several areas in imminent danger of collapse. A survey of the failing foundations educed considerable alarm and it was decided that the building should be rafted and underpinned. Similar concern was generated by the rear elevation and it required the complete rebuilding and re-skinning of the three back walls, using reclaimed 19th century clamp bricks.

Some carved moulding on the Saloon skirting board. All carved woodwork was removed and tanked in a bath of alkaline solution. The paint of centuries came off like pea soup.

By sweeping away the effects of over 200 years the Civic Trust have revealed an internal decoration scheme of outstanding quality and diversity.

Emblems and trophies once dulled with paint now proclaim the virtuosity of the craftsmen who fashioned them and offered a challenge to the present day craftsmen who were used to restore it.

By any standards, the restoration has been an outstanding success, rescuing the house from the brink of collapse. It now takes its place amongst the historical attractions of a rich and varied York, a testament to co-operation and above all to three people who have been passionately involved in York's heritage. Francis Johnson, whose sympathetic restoration is a joy to behold: Noel Terry, whose collection of furniture graces the house with unsurpassed excellence, and above all, John Shannon, Chairman of the York Civic Trust, whose enthusiasm and drive was an inspiration to all.

The principal firms employed on the restoration and selected details of their responsibilities are:

Francis Johnson's designs for the wrought iron panels at the rear of the house.

40

Main Contractors
William Birch & Sons Ltd.,
Foss Islands Road, York.

Joinery
Hare & Ransome,
Heslington Road, York.
Tanking and general repair of all doors and decorative carving. Two mahogany doors for the Saloon and handrail on back stairs.

Painting & Decorating
Bellerbys Ltd.,
35 North Moor Road, Huntington, York.

Electrical
C. R. Manners & Co.,
52A Townsend Street, York.

Plumbing
Tattersall, 63 Walmgate, York.
H. Pickup Ltd.,
Glebe House, Askham Bryan, York.

Wrought Iron
Moorside Wrought Iron,
Piercy End, Kirkbymoorside, York.
Railings and gate on rear elevation. New balustrades on bottom flight of back stairs, lanterns on both staircases.

Repair of Decorative Plaster
Leonard Stead & Son Ltd.,
Victoria Road, Eccleshill, Yorks.

Carving Wood & Stone
Dick Reid,
23 Fishergate, York.
Oculus in front pediment. Replacement carving in Drawing room, Saloon and other parts of the house. New capitals on the Dining room fireplace. Two mahogany beds.

General Stonework & Leadwork
W. M. Anelay Ltd.,
Murton Way, Osbaldwick, York.

Roofing
Joseph Hardgrave Ltd.,
Church Lane, Bishopthorpe, York.

Carpets
Hugh Mackay,
Dragon Lane, Durham.
Dining room, Saloon and Staircase.

Damask
Gainsborough Silk Weaving Co. Ltd.,
Alexandra Road, Chilton,
Sudbury, Suffolk.

Upholstery
Whytock & Reid,
Sunbury House, Belford Mews,
Edinburgh.
Damask hangings, beds.

Upholstery (Chairs)
Rostlea Upholstery Ltd.,
4 Fishergate, Boroughbridge, York.

The original Saloon fireplace removed from the house in 1945. The centre tablet illustrates the conceit of Narcissus.

A replacement fireplace with Siena and Statuary marble in the manner of Henry Cheere.

John Carr

Sir W. Beechey (1753-1839), John Carr c.1785.

John Carr, one of the few provincial architects of the 18th century to attain national importance, was born at Horbury near Wakefield the son of a stonemason.

He spent most of his life living and working in York of which he was twice Lord Mayor and it was in this city that he consolidated his reputation when his design for the York grandstand on the Knavesmire racecourse was chosen in preference to one by James Paine. The building was completed in 1754 and was generally admitted to be remarkably well adapted to its intended purposes, a comment that could be made about most of Carr's houses and in general it was appreciated by owners who were 'indebted for the comforts and elegancies of their buildings'[47].

In his early practice he came into contact with Lord Burlington during the construction of Kirby Hall for Stephen Thompson 1747-c.55 and this Palladian influence stayed with him throughout his career. Carr proved in later years that he could adopt the neoclassical style to great

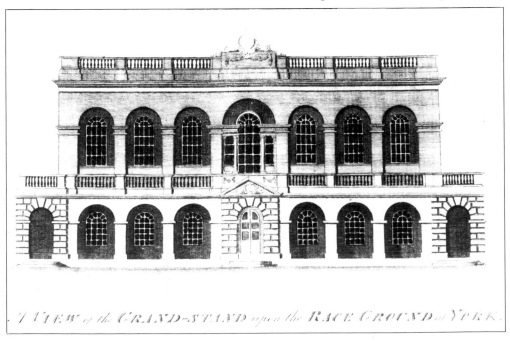

A VIEW of the GRAND-STAND upon the RACE GROUND at YORK.

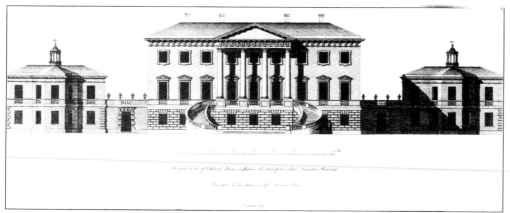

Tabley House (formerly named Oaklands) Vitruvius Britannicus, Vol.5, p.19.

Old Entrance Hall. Stucco medallions celebrate the so called Aldbrandini Marriage (A 1st century A.D. Roman fresco found on the Esquiline in 1604/5) after drawings by Poussin and Angelica Kauffmann.

Drawing room (formerly Dining room). The fireplace came from York, probably supplied by the Fisher family. It is strikingly similar to that supplied for the Saloon at Fairfax House in 1760-62.

effect, but his early work showed an innate conservatism and restraint that must have appealed to his predominantly Yorkshire clientele.

Of all his buildings, perhaps Tabley House near Knutsford is the clearest example of his continuing adherence to the traditions of palladianism despite a close involvement with Robert Adam and Harewood House at the same time.

Like William Kent he planned his rooms in the same way that a garden would be landscaped. The chance to create a sense of spatial excitement was irresistible. Dominant features would be strategically placed to catch the eye such as a garden statue standing at the end of a shaded walk, but above all he was an architect who created buildings for people to live in and it was observed by Dr Whitaker that 'in the designs of houses, Mr Carr was eminently happy: no-one had more studied or more thoroughly understood the arrangement and proportion of private apartments, nor are his elevations devoid of grace and symmetry'.

Carr's competence as an architect was respected in the most sophisticated circles and his election to the London Architects' Club (he was the only provincial member) ensured his continuing success.

Coving of the Library ceiling at Fairfax House.

When Woolfe and Gandon's fifth volume of *Vitruvius Britannicus* was published in 1771, there were 15 plates devoted to Carr's work, compared to only 12 of William Kent's, 9 of Robert Adam's and 3 of Sir William Chambers. A great tribute to an architect only half way through his career and this high esteem was to continue, for the same prominence was evident some 30 years later in Richardson's two volumes of *New Vitruvius Britannicus*. The first volume published in 1862 had nine plates of Carr's work compared to the Adam brothers 10. No other leading architect – neither Mylne, Holland, Bonomi, Soane, Cockerell, Leverton or Stuart were allotted more than five plates, whilst in the second volume of 1808 Carr was given pride of place at the very front with his design for the Assize Courts at York an honour equal to that given to the Horse Guards, Greenwich Hospital and St. Paul's Cathedral in earlier volumes[48].

Newburgh Priory. Stucco by G. Cortese, c.1740.

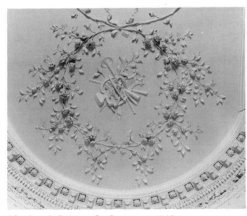

Newburgh Priory, G. Cortese, c.1765.

Heath Hall, Wakefield. Drawing room. Stuccowork probably by Joseph Rose, the elder, c.1758.

Heath Hall, Drawing room.

He was a traditionalist at heart, but not dogmatic and the basic character of Carr's architecture could sometimes be modified by the influence of his favourite plasterers, men able to introduce the spirit of the Rococo into designs for the stucco. Perhaps the most successful of these was Guiseppe Cortese a native of Lugano in Switzerland who settled in Yorkshire and lived there until his death in 1778. He worked on many occasions in conjunction with the York plasterer James Henderson and on the death of Thomas Perritt in 1759, reigned supreme for over a decade as the leading stuccoist in the North[49].

There are numerous houses in Yorkshire that have their stucco attributed to Cortese but sadly the family papers of many of these have crucial gaps in their sequence, almost as if an early researcher on the works of John Carr has extracted these papers from the various archives. Fortunately there is sufficient evidence in the form of daybooks and ledger entries to overcome this problem and it allows some attribution on more than just stylistic grounds.

It is of particular interest therefore to compare the work of Cortese carried out in 1744 and again in 1767 at Newburgh Priory, home of the Earls Fauconberg in the 18th century. The designs had become much more naturalistic 20 years on and they provide a useful register when comparing the stucco at Fairfax House with that seen in other houses where Cortese's input is evident.

Castlegate House, Drawing room, Daniel Shillitoe, c.1763.

The fireplace was another vital component in the decoration of a room, being the first object that strikes the eye on entrance and the most conspicuous part of the room. This principle was well known to Carr who put much thought into his designs for chimney pieces.

He preferred to patronise local carvers and masons rather than the more expensive Cheere family of Hyde Park Corner in London. At Tabley House the marble chimney pieces were procured by Carr from York probably from the Fisher family, whilst those fashioned in wood were supplied by his favourite carver Daniel Shillitoe[50]. Shillitoe, like Cortese, established his workshop in Wakefield and by 1761 he had at least two apprentices, Matthew Ward and John Richardson, working for him. Both had carried out commissions at Fairfax House carving roses for the underside of the great staircase, whilst at Tabley House a Matthew Bertram is recorded as assisting Shillitoe in his work.

Most of the decorative woodwork at Heath Hall near Wakefield had been fashioned by Shillitoe and the same hand

Heath Hall, South-west bedroom, Daniel Shillitoe, c.1762.

Castlegate House, Drawing room, Shillitoe, c.1763.

can be seen at work in Fairfax House, Castlegate House, Everingham and Harewood. The patterns used for the mouldings fall into distinct categories, the most popular being variations of the traditional egg, shell and dart theme where the pattern is repeated on the window architrave and on the skirting board. Other designs utilise a symmetrical arrangement of husk and raffle leaf and in the principal rooms the mouldings are often enriched with scrolled medallions

fashion both staircases and was also commissioned to create an elegant set of railings for the front[51]. Sadly these were swept away in 1879 when Castlegate was widened, but Ridsdale Tate, an architect working next door made a sketch of these before they were demolished.

Tobin was perhaps the leading northern smith of his generation. More information on his influence has yet to come to light but he was certainly commissioned to make a free standing

Great Staircase balusters by Maurice Tobin, c.1762.

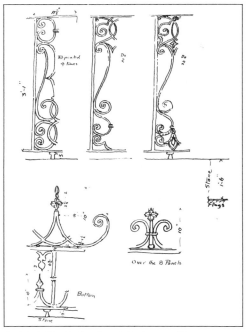

Ridsdale Tate's sketches of the front railings, 1878.

enclosing stylised waves, foliage and husks. The greatest effort usually went into the overdoor details however and presumably Shillitoe and his team were allowed much more freedom in which to display their considerable talents.

The other medium that Carr used to great effect was his wrought iron work and in this he was helped on many occasions by the Leeds whitesmith and wrought-iron worker Maurice Tobin. At Fairfax House, Tobin had been used to

stove for Edward Lascelles at Harewood using a mahogany pattern provided by Thomas Chippendale[52] and he was also required to provide the grates for the fireplaces, a commission he also undertook at Tabley.

Balustrades were his speciality however and he had worked to Carr's designs for the Dundas family at Aske Hall, at Norton Place in Lincolnshire and at Constable Burton, the home of Sir Marmaduke Wyvill.

A cast 'busto' by John Cheere, ex: Kirkleatham Collection

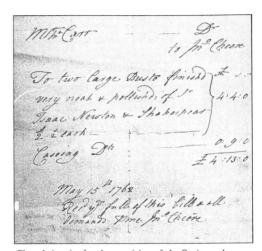

Cheere's invoice for the provision of the Staircase busts.

Carr's reputation rested on his ability to please his many customers and no commission was considered too small or troublesome. In 1765, just two years after Fairfax House was completed he went through the house with the painter to assess the state of decoration. The following letter reveals his common sense attitude and attention to detail.

'To The Right Honorable Ld. Fairfax at Gilling Castle near Easingwold

My Lord

I have been through your house today with the Painter to see what is necessary to be done, and if it is agreeable to your Lordship have determined he shall paint the Great Dining Room and Parlour Cornices but not the Ceilings; Also the Drawing Room Cornice and Ceiling and Miss Fairfax dressing Room Cornice and Ceiling, and the Stair Case Cornice and Ceiling which are very dirty.

Pentiman will finish the whole of his work about the Coach house and Hot house on Monday next, we have dug a Vault in the lower part under the Coach house and arched it to receive the Surplus Rain water from the top at one end, and at the other end have carried the water into the Lane next to Mr Wauds. The lead cistern is placed in the Hot house and all the inside finished but the Door hanging which I find is not yet made nor the Coach house doors but have sent to Robinson to get them done immediately. I hope we shall soon see the stone come for the pillars after which the yard may be levelled. As the wall opposite the Great Staircase window looks disagreeable I think it would be the cheapest and neatest to run a coat of stucco up and plant some flowering shrubs against the low part of it, but this I want your Lordship approbation of before I give orders about it.

I am my Lord on all occasions your Lordships most obedient and most humble servant Jon Carr

York 15th June 1765'

Carr was not above making mistakes however. The pillars referred to in the letter as supplied by Shillitoe were six in number, and when set in place in front of the new coach house they proved to be 'disagreeable'. He sought the Viscount's permission to reduce this to four and suggested that the other two could be used to good effect at Gilling castle. Hoping no doubt that he would not be required to carry the cost of this extra stonework himself.

A Tour of the House

Fairfax House has been described as a classic architectural masterpiece of its age and certainly one of the finest townhouses in England. It was saved from near collapse by the York Civic Trust and restored to its former glory during 1982/84.

To all intents and purposes it was 'lost to the City' says the Trust Chairman, John Shannon. 'Of course, we knew about the house, but a building which in the 20th century had become an adjunct of a cinema and later leased as a dance hall, was inevitably being ignored and overlooked, its superb virtues forgotten by most people but happily not by the York Civic Trust. Our intention has been to restore the house to its rightful place in York's Heritage' he says.

In addition, the famous Noel G. Terry Collection was given to the Trust for display in the house and has been described by Christie's as one of the finest private collections of 18th century English furniture and clocks formed this century.

Together with paintings, rugs and chinese porcelain it provides the basis for what can now be considered a fully furnished Georgian Townhouse.

The Trust have retained the cinema's glazed terracotta portico as an entrance to the shop and reception area. Access to the first room in Fairfax House is gained from here through a modern jib door, decorated with a door-case rescued from Stillington Hall near York.

Exterior

The shell of the house dates from about 1745 having a front elevation with a symmetrical 5 x 3 arrangement. The centre section is surmounted by a pediment and has an oculus within its spandrel. A portico modified in the 19th century is fitted in the middle of the ground floor and the stone architraves of the windows and the quoins, although previously rusticated, have been hacked back at some time due to the poor quality of stone used.

To the left a late Georgian house was converted into a cinema entrance in the 1920s and the company's remodelling of the facade involved a continuation of the stone bands separating the floors and the creation of windows with the same pulvinated friezes.

Interior

A richly decorated interior completed in 1762 by Carr of York for the Roman Catholic peer Viscount Fairfax and his daughter Anne displays some of the finest plasterwork and carved woodwork in Yorkshire. The designs range from the rococo work of the entrance and staircase to the more naturalistic forms of the Dining Room and Saloon and typify the kind of work carried out in this transitional period before the designs of Robert Adam became so popular.

Noel Terry's collection of furniture and clocks is arranged throughout the house in as logical a manner as possible. He had made no effort to assemble the balanced furnishings of an 18th century interior and therefore the collection is displayed in a less formal 20th century manner.

All contents are listed from the left when standing and facing the fireplace.

Library

Ceiling
A lightly compartmented ceiling with tied medallions of crossed palm leaves and garlands of flowers decorating the coving. In the centre, four portrait medallions of John Milton, Joseph Addison, John Locke and Alexander Pope are set in oak leaf garlands and surround an octagonal centre section enriched with a symmetrical arrangement of interlinking strapwork and foliage.

Decoration
Scrapes revealed that all carved woodwork and stucco between the dado and skirting board had been painted a light stone colour and that the walls were given a flat straw yellow tone that was intended presumably to complement the Siena marble used in the fireplace. Colour sections on the doors showed a dark chocolate ground but it was difficult to determine whether or not they had been veined to simulate mahogany.

Fireplace
One of the two fireplaces to survive occupation by the cinema company.

Siena and statuary marble set with a Greek key pattern in the frieze and fitted with a later grate.

Woodwork
Window architrave . . strapwork pattern intended to complement the ceiling. Doorcase . . Pulvinated frieze of mixed acanthus with a plain centre tablet. The shell and flower pattern on the architrave is repeated in the design of the skirting board.

Pictures
School of G. P. Pannini (c. 1692-1765). Figures set against a capriccio of classical ruins.
Signed *E.A.S.* (?). Portrait of a boy.
W. Van Mieris (1662-1747). Portrait of a Gentleman.
Jacobus Janson (1729-1784). Said to be the Painted Chamber, Westminster.
Thomas Wyck. Figures in a courtyard.
Andrew Festing, 1985, after Sir W. Beechey. Portrait of John Carr.
J. Janson. Painted Chamber, Westminster.
Pieter van Slingelandt (1640-1691). Man and woman in an interior.
Gonzales Coques (1618-1684). Lady with a parrot.
Jonathan Richardson (1665-1745). Portrait of the artist.
Pieter van der Werff (1665-1721). Gentleman on a terrace.
J.J. van Goyen (1595-1666). Pair of pencil and grey wash sketches of a seashore.
John Closterman (1656-1713). Said to be Sir Richard Temple of Stowe.

Clocks
Longcase Clock c.1685-90, month going, by Thomas Tompion. 10 inch square dial with anchor escapement. ex: Lowther Castle.

Furniture

Torchere, rosewood, c.1755. Baluster column and shallow tray top.

Artist's Table, mahogany, c.1755. Double rising top worked by ratchet brackets.

Bureau Bookcase, mahogany, c.1775. Att. to the workshop of Thomas Chippendale. Drawers have ivory inlaid letters and lions' mask handles.

Cistern Stand, mahogany and bronze, c.1810, in Egyptian style. Base holds removable water container.

Chair, one of two, c.1740, mahogany with petit-point needlework seat. ex: Lord Savile, Rufford Abbey. Vase shaped splat and scallop-shell cresting.

Armchair, mahogany, c.1750, scrolled toes and acanthus leaf decoration.

Armchair, walnut, c.1725. Lions' masks on the knee and having club feet.

Sofa Table, mahogany, c.1815. Inlaid with coromandel crossbanding.

Writing Case, mahogany, c.1800. Beaded metal edging.

Music Stand, mahogany, c.1820. Popularly referred to as a Canterbury.

Bellows, walnut, c.1580. Mannerist faces and figures symbolise the elements.

Bureau Bookcase, mahogany, c.1790. Gothic taste.

Writing Table, mahogany, c.1755, after a design by Thomas Chippendale. A long drawer in the frieze pulls out for writing.

Carved box, walnut, c.1735, shows Polish Kings from AD 550 to 1733.

Tripod Table, mahogany, c.1760. Tilting occasional table with 'pie-crust' edge.

Chandelier, bronze & glass, c.1830. Originally fitted with an oil lamp.

Ceramics

Brinjal Bowls, 2 and 1, yellow ground, Kangxi (1662-1722).

Brushwater & Waterpot, modelled as a lotus leaf and decorated with crustacea in relief, Kangxi.

Carp, famille verte biscuit figure leaping from the waves, Kangxi.

Saucer Dish, one of two, Chinese Imari, Qianlong (1736-1795).

Carpets

Tekke Turkoman, columns of ghuls and wide sunburst lozenge border. Kilim strips and pole straps on one edge.

Serapi runner, blue field with diagonal rows of boteh in an ivory floral border. Skittle pattern stripes and plain outer border.

Statuary

John Carr, after a bust by Nollekens

Exit through the door into the corridor.

Entrance Hall

The principal entrance to the house retains its original oak doors and gives access to Carr's carefully contrived vista of arches.

Ceiling

The restrained ceiling and its delicate cornicing is very much in keeping with the Palladian concept of the crescendo. The centre 'cabbage' roundel is edged with a vitruvian scroll and there are secondary panels of interlinking C scrolls joined at the centre by rose and foliate medallions.

The arches are supported on enriched pilasters and have, like the entrance hall in Castlegate House opposite, some unusual acanthus capitals.

Floor
A replacement of Elland slabs with Welsh slate insets arranged in a traditional Yorkshire pattern.

Decoration
In 1762 Samuel Carpenter quoted '3d a yard three times neatly done' to paint the stucco. He also quoted for the woodwork to be done with a gloss paint, but this would be more of a silk or eggshell finish than the modern hard gloss that we know today.

Woodwork
A pair of door surrounds with mouldings that have similar patterns to the library architrave but with pulvinated friezes that mirror the designs in the ceiling.

The skirting board is edged with a flower and ribbon twist carving that is carried on up the great staircase.

Pictures
Johannes Storck (fl. 1660-1680). A pair of Dutch canal scenes.

Furniture
Chest of Drawers, paint and lacquer, c.1795. English version of a Japanese technique.
Chair, one of two, mahogany, c.1780. Decorated in the Gothic taste.

Clocks
Bracket Clock, c.1665, by Edward East of London (1602-1698). Case is of ebonised pearwood, the 8-day movement has a pivoted verge escapement.

Barometers
Ivory free standing Barometer, c.1695, in the manner of Daniel Quare (1649-1724).
Walnut syphon tube wheel Barometer, c.1755, by George Hallifax of Doncaster (1725-1811).
Mahogany syphon tube Barometer, c.1785, by John Agar, Castlegate, York. ex: Y. Lloyd-Greame, Esq., Sewerby House, Bridlington.
Mahogany Barometer, c.1790, by Charles Polti, Exeter (d.1792). A cistern tube with screw adjustment, together with an alcohol thermometer and a hygrometer intended to register humidity.

Entering the Dining room on the right.

Dining Room

Ceiling
A centre medallion of Abundantia taken from a design in the pattern book *Iconologia* by Cesare Ripa, 5th edition, c.1645, with secondary displays of musical instruments at her head and crossed wine glasses and church wardens' pipes at her feet. Baskets of fruit and flowers in the corners represent the seasons and bordering the whole ceiling is a cornice whose design is based on the Doric order of Albano. These groups of inverted cones, called guttae, are often used on an external cornice as in the case of Castlegate House opposite, or as an embellishment for an entrance hall.

Restoration involved over 1,000 man hours of painstaking cleaning and scraping on this ceiling alone. The stucco decoration however proved to be in suprisingly good condition despite being directly below a dancehall and a leaking cloakroom for over fifty years.

Woodwork

A highly individual decorative scheme with elaborate doorcases supporting lavishly carved broken pediments. The egg, flower and shell pattern is repeated on the window architrave and both dado and skirting are enriched with stylised husks and foliage.

Fireplace

The only other fireplace to survive in situ. New capitals were carved for the columns and a replacement tablet fashioned to portray Aesop's fable of the Wolf and the Crane. The columns are a rare pink and cream marble (probably a form of Felspar) and the chimneypiece may well have been supplied by Henry Cheere of Hyde Park.

Decoration

Scrapes revealed an initial coat of blue/green paint which when reproduced, had little sympathy with the polychrome fireplace. This may have been intended as a dark ground undercoat for a lighter colour scheme and decoration proceeded on this assumption.

Pictures

Sir Peter Lely (1618-1680). Elizabeth Uvedale, 2nd Countess of Carlisle. On loan from Castle Howard.

Hermel van Steenwyck (fl.1644-58). Still life with a parrot.

Abraham Storck (1630-1710). Dutch two-deckers in a choppy sea.

Jan van der Bent (1650-1690). Capriccio of a Mediterranean harbour.

Jacob Marel (1614-1685). A still life of flowers and insects.

Willem van de Velde, the elder (1610-1693). The Dromedary & United Provinces, painted en grisaille.

P. van Host (1707?). The village school.

Artist unknown, English, c.1695. Admiral Robert Fairfax. On loan from York City Art Gallery.

School of Jan Evert Morel (1777-1808). Still life of fruit and flowers.

Furniture

Torchères, one of two, mahogany, c.1760. Attributed to the workshops of Thomas Chippendale. ex: The Earl Howe, Penn House, Bucks.

Spinet, walnut, dated 17th July 1769. Made by John Kirsham, Manchester.

Stool, walnut, c. 1720. Cabriole legs and petit-point needlework seat.

Torchères, one of two, mahogany, c.1765. Circular tops and spindle gallery.

Tripod Table, mahogany, c.1755. A hinged octagonal top and pierced tripod base after designs by Ince & Mayhew.

Cutlery Case, one of two, mahogany, c.1800. Rising tops with gadrooned carving and trailing pendants of husks on the base.

Sideboard, mahogany, c.1810. Incorporates a chamber pot cupboard at the side.

Two-tier Table, mahogany, c.1755. Highly accomplished dumb-waiter with revolving octagonal tiers and pierced gallery.

Chair, one of four, mahogany, c.1760. A popular 'Owls-eye' splat with a hint of Gothic tracery at the base.

Dressing Cabinet, mahogany, c.1760-65. The top drawer pulls out for writing and for use as a dressing table.

Plate Buckets, mahogany and brass, c.1800. Carved with diagonal reeding.

Bureau Cabinet, mahogany, c.1770. The fall front secretaire section is supported on quadrant brackets.

Mirror, gilded pine, Queen Anne style. On loan from York City Art Gallery.

Table, walnut, c.1730. Kneehole recess for writing or dressing. Boldly carved cabriole legs with hairy paw feet.

Cheese Coaster, mahogany, c.1790.

Dining Table, mahogany, c.1775. Elaborately carved frieze with swagged garlands and baskets of fruit.

Chair, one of eight and one carver, mahogany, c.1760-70. Ladderback dining chairs with curved seats.

Chair, mahogany, c.1765, after a design in Chippendale's *'Director'.*

Clocks

Longcase Clock, c.1670, 8-day, by Edward East, London (1602-1698). A 10 inch square dial with solid silver chapter ring and anchor escapement. The walnut case has a rising hood with twist turned columns and an octagonal lenticle in the door that allows sight of the pendulum.

Bracket Clock, c.1680, by Joseph Knibb (active in London 1670-97). An 8-day movement with verge escapement set in an ebony case.

Carpet

Rectangular Wilton carpet, 'Turkey' pattern, Hugh Mackay of Durham.

Ceramics

The majority of porcelain on display formed part of the now famous 'Nanking Cargo', c.1751, rescued from the wreck of the 'Geldermalsen' discovered in the South China Seas by Capt. Michael Hatcher and Max De Rham.

Silver

The group arranged on the dining table and sideboard have been bought in memory of Leslie Boothman and Arthur Smallwood whose wills provided funds for the acquisition of silver for Fairfax House. They form the core of the bequest but will be supplemented with other items as and when they become available.

A George II eight-branch epergne, by William Cripps, 1757, 36cm high (157ozs). Standing on four shell and scroll feet, each with detachable leaf-capped scroll branches terminating in octagonal candle sockets. The oval frame has an applied apron pierced and chased with foliage and dragons and with four detachable branches each terminating in a detachable circular sweetmeat dish.

The arms are probably those of Dyke of Horsham, Sussex, probably for Anne Dyke, widow of Sir Thomas Dyke of Lullingstone Castle, Co. Devon, who died in 1756.

A set of four George III candlesticks, by Daniel Smith and Robert Sharp, 1761, 27cm high (100ozs). They each stand on stepped square gadrooned bases with a baluster stem, spool-shaped socket, fluted detachable square nozzles and gadrooned borders, the stems later engraved with a monogram.

A pair of George II sauceboats, by Frederick Kandler, 1747, 21cm long (50ozs). They are supported on spreading oval feet cast with shells and scrolls, the scalloped rim similarly applied and with leaf-capped scroll handles.

A pair of George III two-handled oval soup tureens and covers by Thomas Robins, 1807, 40cm long overall (296ozs). Resting on four lions mask, claw and ball feet with shell and foliage scroll handles and shell and gadrooned everted rims.

The arms are those of Ellis, Southside, Scotland impaling another.

A set of ten dinner plates, by John Mortimer and John S. Hunt, 1839, 24cm diameter (178ozs). Each plate is engraved with the arms of Middleton quartering Noel impaling Jocelyn, for Charles Noel, 1st Earl of Gainsborough (1781-1866).

A set of Hanoverian pattern cutlery, by C. J. Vander, 1990 (124 pieces in all).

A shaped-circular salver, by Thomas Hannam and John Crouch, 1803, 57cm diameter (192ozs). Standing on four massive lion's paw feet with a cast and pierced border decorated with bacchanalian masks, trailing vines, shells, insects and snails. At the centre is the Royal Coat of Arms. From the collection of The Rt. Hon. The Viscountess d'Abernon.

Exit through the second door into the staircase lobby.

Staircase Lobby

Ceiling

The heavily compartmented ceiling ribs are decorated with a guilloche pattern and they enclose two foliate roundels. Enriched console brackets form a conclusion for the cornice and provide an elegant solution to a difficult architectural problem.

Stucco Panel

The oval stucco medallion with its swagged drapery and trailing pendant illustrates the goddess Roma, after an engraving in P. A. Maffei's, *Gemme Antiche Figurate*, (1707-09). She holds a winged victory in her hand and is attended by a goat. Support is provided by some sheep and trailing from the base is a garland of roses.

It may be that the Viscount was using this classical representation as a 'nod' in the direction of his religion. The only other recorded use of this engraved source in stucco is at Riverstown House Co. Cork in Ireland, the 18th century home of Dr. Jemmet Browne, Lord Bishop of Cork.

Woodwork

The guilloche pattern of the ceiling is repeated on the three overdoor panels whilst the architrave has a delicate tracery of leaf and husks. Observe the characteristic concave profile where the moulding joins the flat architrave. This is one of Carr's favourite techniques and utilises the play of light and shade to create an illusion of greater depth.

Staircase

Excessive use by the cinema company caused many of the cantilevered stairs to break where they join the wall and cast replacements were necessary. Most of the carved flowers however, set on the underside of each step and provided by Shillitoe's apprentices, have been re-used. Maurice Tobin's balustrading and the mahogany handrail required very little repair. The removal of a sweet kiosk in the stairwell resulted in the building of new steps and a side entrance.

Paintings

Andrew Festing, 1985. Retrospective portrait of Noel G. Terry shown against a backdrop of the Merchant Adventurers' Hall and the Terry Chocolate Factory.

School of F. van Mieris (1635-81). Portrait of a gentleman in silk ruffs.

Furniture

Chair, walnut, c.1705. Elaborate fishscale decoration, trellis hatching and husks in imitation of Chinese designs.

Chest of Drawers, mahogany, c.1765. Serpentine front and canted corners carved with foliate pendants. ex: Bramshill Park.

Chest of Drawers, mahogany and satinwood, c.1770. Top drawer converts to dressing table.

Sedan Chair, painted leather, c.1830.

Clocks

Longcase Clock, c.1775, by Robert Anderson, Liverpool. A 12 inch arched dial shows phases of the moon. Mahogany case richly carved with pierced columns on a scrolled broken pediment surmounted by eagle finials.

Regulator Clock, c.1790. James Boynton, Howden, Yorks.

Ceramics
A late Ming blue and white *'Kraak Porselein'* dish painted with an insect amongst foliage, Wanli (1573-1619).
A large *Delft* blue and white vase, monogrammed VE, early 18th century.

Exit to the rear stairs and turn left.

Kitchen

A re-created kitchen in what was probably the rear parlour. The original servants' wing had been demolished in 1920 by the cinema company to make way for their auditorium. All the food on display is modelled to reproduce a meal given by the Viscount Fairfax on April 15th, 1763.

Metalwork
A late-18th century deep draught fire by Green's of Halifax. The smoke-jack spit is driven by the hot air rising and turning a fan in the chimney. This drives the bevel gears and operates both vertical and horizontal spits. On either side a bread oven and hotplate are both heated by their own firebox.

Items accompanying the fire include a chimney crane, ratchet hooks, hooks and racks, trivets, griddle, boiling pot, kettle, digester, dip tray and basting spoon.

Copper and Brass
Set of copper pans. ex: Judge's Lodgings.
Late-18th century Warming Pan - water filled.
19th century Warming Pan - coal filled with wooden handle.
Jelly Moulds, Cream Jug, Toasting Fork and Milk Skimmer.
19th century Muffin Warmer with concertina handle.

Pewter
Various Plates and Plate Warmers, 18th and 19th century.
Venison Tray, late-18th century.
Coffee Kettles and Milk Jugs, early-18th century.

Furniture
Chair, one of two, mahogany, c.1785. Provincial 'Chippendale' pattern.
Dole Cupboard, oak, c.1750. Provincial food press.
Chair, walnut and oak, c.1730. An early Windsor pattern.
Table, pine, the top is hinged on one side and converts to a bench seat. This type is sometimes referred to as a 'Monk-seat' but this expression is incomprehensible.
Linen Press, walnut and oak, c.1690.
Dough Trough, oak, splayed legs and tapered sides.
Dresser, pine, base c.1750, with modern plate rack.

Clock
Longcase Clock, c.1760, by Joseph Hallifax of Barnsley. Late-18th and early-19th century illustrations of country house interiors show similar longcase clocks in the kitchen.
cf: Caroline Davidson, *The World of Mary Ellen Best,* 1985, p.29.

Miscellanea
Bread Peel, Bellows, Spittle, Ladles, Potato Masher, Spatula, Roller and Oatcake Spreader.
Sugar Loaf and Sugar Scissors, Pestle and Mortar, Colander.
Butter Bowl and Scotch Hands.
Glass Smoothing Irons, used to put the shine back on the pressed Damask or Linen.

Retrace your steps.

Rear Staircase

Offered the only access to the guest bedrooms and long gallery on the top floor. The bottom flight had been removed and replacement is based on the pattern of the surviving flights.

Metalwork
Balustrades by Maurice Tobin, Leeds, 1761. The leading north country Smith of his generation.

Furniture

Chair, one of two, walnut, c.1695. Strong affinity to the designs of Daniel Marot.
Writing Bureau, walnut, c.1710.
Buffet, oak, c.1610. Often seen illustrated with a garnish of pewter.
Panel, oak and lime, c.1690, in the manner of Grinling Gibbons.

Textiles

Carpet, Kashan prayer rug, c.1910. Blood red baluster vase set in a tan field, flanked with flowering trees.
Carpet, Kashan prayer rug, embossed silk, c.1910. A vase and bouquet of flowers is surmounted by a flowering tree of life with cavorting deer and Hoopoe birds.

Ceramics

Three large saucer dishes and a baluster shaped vase, in famille verte colours, late Kangxi (1662-1722).

Ascending the rear staircase to the first floor landing.

Paintings

Artist unknown, English, c.1750. Beilby Thompson Esq. of Escrick Hall.
J. W. Carmichael (1800-1868). Shipping offshore in a choppy sea, dated 1845.
Artist unknown, English, c.1740. Dame Francis Hardies, wife of Sir William.

Artist unknown, English, c.1740. Sir William Hardies Bt.
Artist unknown, English, c.1780. Oval portrait of lady in red. Reputed to have come from Gilling Castle.
Thomas Hudson (1701-1770). Portrait of Archbishop Thomas Herring, dated 1743.

Textiles

Carpet, Koum Ka Pour prayer rug, silk and metal thread, c.1900. Unusual to find living creatures woven into the design of Turkish Mohammedan rugs.

Statuary

J. Fisher. Marble medallion of putti and goat, c.1834, reputedly intended for an unfinished fireplace at Duncombe Park, Yorkshire.

Anne's Bedroom

One of only two bedrooms on the first floor. Decorated with a 'Mock India' paper from the Temple Newsam Collection that reflects the daughter's choice in 1762. The walls had also been trimmed with a gold fillet and this may be carried out at a later date.

During the occupancy of the cinema company the room had been used for refreshments with an extra entrance to the dancehall being created in the West wall. Windows had been blocked in and all fireplaces on the first floor removed and sold off.

Ceiling

A delicate stepped cornice with foliage garlands and rose medallions set below a narrow moulding of shell and flower.

Fireplace

Carved wood and marble with elaborate Carron grate, c.1770. ex: Methley Hall, Wakefield.

Woodwork

A vigorous pulvinated frieze with flowing scrolls and rose medallions. The architrave is more restrained and repeats the foliate decoration on the skirting.

No trace of the dado rail remained but it may well have carried the same egg and dart pattern seen in the Viscount's bedroom.

Paintings

H.J. Dubbels (fl.1650?). Dutch Shipping.
Bartolome Estaban Murillo (1617-1682). Cupid asleep on a cross.
Attributed to Philip Mercier (1689-1760). Portrait of Anne Fairfax as a shepherdess. ex: Newburgh Priory. Instead of a shepherd's crook she holds a houlette, a spoon shaped tool for throwing stones.
Artist unknown, English, c.1700. Oval portrait of Lady Anne Spencer (Mary Beale).

Artist unknown. Portrait *miniature* of a Cardinal. ex: Hotham Hall, Howden.

Furniture

Dressing Commode, mahogany, c.1760. Attributed to the workshops of Thomas Chippendale. ex: Dukes of Manchester.
Tallboy Secretaire, mahogany, c.1765, of north country origin.
Writing Table, mahogany, c.1760. Central sliding cupboard pushes back to create the kneehole recess.
Dressing Bureau, mahogany, c.1735. Carved lions' masks at the knee and hairy paw feet.
Chair, mahogany, c.1755. Pre-Director design with pierced splat and dolphins' feet.
Secretaire, mahogany, c.1760. The pierced shelving in the Gothic taste, is intended for the display of china.
Bedsteps, mahogany, c.1820. Middle step pulls out as a night commode.
Four-poster Bed, mahogany. The tester is fashioned from some carved pelmets c.1750 made by G. Reynoldson of York and rescued from Kilnwick. Upholstered in an Italian Moire silk by Whytock & Reid, Edinburgh.

Ceramics

Bowl, with overted rim and decorated in famille verte colours with butterflies, fruit and flowers, 19th century.
Bowl, with lightly fluted rim and decorated with bats, fruit and flowers in famille verte colours, 19th century.
Armorial Bowl, one of two, deeply fluted rim in famille rose colours, possibly Dutch.
Ribbed Saucer-dish, one of two, famille verte painted with flowers, pheasants and foliage, Kangxi (1662-1722).
Vase, quatrefoil shape on famille verte colours, yellow loop handles, Kangxi.
Part Wash Set, Spode Copeland. Peony pattern jugs, basins and soap dish, 19th century. ex: Harewood House.
Standing Boy, one of two, famille verte figures holding vases of flowers in opposite hands, Kangxi.
Plate, edged with a Persian flute and decorated in famille verte colours.
Soup Bowl, in famille verte colours.
Soup Bowl, decorated with lattice fence and fighting cocks in famille verte colours.
Teapot, famille verte colours and deep blue tracery, Kangxi.
Teapot, redware, c.1850 with applied foliate decoration in 17th century style.

Textiles

Hamadan runner, c.1920, with brown field and seven linked serrated lozenges.
Bokhara runner, with ruby field and linked octagons, modern.
Bokhara carpet, with blue field and double row of octagons, modern.

Miscellanea

Joshua Stopford, *Ways and methods of Romes Advancement,* 1675.
Institute of S. Marie, *Introduction à la Vie Devote de Saint Francois de Sales,* 1685. Signed Mary Fairfax, younger sister of Anne.
Purse, yellow silk, c.1880.
Candlestick, plated c.1885 with its original wick trimmer.
Rosary, 1873, souvenir of Lourdes.
Plaque, bronzed plaster of Jesus Christ.
Cross, ivory & ebony, c.1900, in the Jensenist manner.
Brushes, silver, Birmingham 1910.
Fire-irons, brass, c.1900.

Exit out of the bedroom and turn right onto the main staircase landing.

Great Staircase

Described as an architectural masterpiece of its age and a model example of an 18th century hall set in a townhouse that is located on a restricted site.

Ceiling
A superb display of the 18th century taste for allegory proclaiming on the one hand, a support for King and country with its strong military theme, a risky allegiance to the Roman Catholic cause and a dangerous support of the Jacobite cause.

The centre medallion is of *'Architettura Militare'* another of Ripa's representations. The design has been personalised to please the Viscount, however, for Cortese has introduced a fortress into the design and a Union Jack flies from the flag pole.

In the coving, warlike animals and beasts jostle for place with weapons of the military, whilst a putto clutching an armful of arrows and bolts of thunder declaims the power of eloquence to those ascending the stairs. Opposite, another putto holds a flaming torch in one hand and can be said to be casting light on the 'true' religion.

Walls
Crossed palm leaves and swagged drapery form a setting for some console brackets supporting busts of Sir Isaac Newton and William Shakespear (sic). An enlightened concept in the 18th century to consider the arts and sciences as two distinct subjects.

Window
A Serlian or Venetian window with marble columns above a stone balustrade. The window had been bricked in by the Cinema Company and glazed with opaque glass to hide the bricks.

Heraldry
The Viscount's arms (Fairfax of Emley) show an Argent (silver) field with 3 bars gemelles gules (red) overall a lion rampant sable (black). In the crest a lion passant sable. The family motto on the ribbon below, *Je le Feray Durant ma Vie*, loosely translated as 'I will accomplish it in my lifetime'.

Ironwork
The principal element of the balustrade is a figure-eight shaped panel formed by some intersecting scrolls and having a central lozenge with stamped double roses.

Three of the panels on the landing differ from the rest by the introduction of double rosebuds in the upper and lower sections and may well be a further testimony to the Viscount's support of the Jacobite cause.

Woodwork
Highly accomplished set of overdoors carved in pine and showing some swagged garlands of fruit and flowers.

The carved moulding of the architrave has an unusual cupped egg and flower pattern and the scrolled brackets supporting the cornice are enriched with fan and flower.

Of the four doors on the landing, three are painted pine and one mahogany.

Decoration
It took over 1,000 man hours to remove the dark blue and dark red gloss paint from the walls and ceilings.

Carpet
A modern Wilton 'yardage' carpet edged with a border that repeats various patterns on the stairs. By Hugh Mackay of Durham.

Furniture

Chair, one of two, mahogany, c.1755. A pre-Director design with elaborately pierced splat, bold cabriole legs and standing on dolphins' feet.

Clock

Longcase Clock, c.1685, by Henry Jones of London (active 1663-1695). A 10 inch square dial with skeletonised chapter-ring set against a matted background. The walnut case has a rising hood secured by a spoon lock which is only released when the trunk door is opened.

Turn left off the landing into the second bedroom.

Viscount's Bedroom

In 1762 the Viscount had a clear view over his kitchen garden to the River Foss. By 1920 however, the room was converted into ladies' and gentlemen's toilets as an adjunct to the dancehall.

Decoration

A daisy pattern wallpaper, one of the papers exhibited at the Temple Newsam Exhibition of Historic Wallcoverings in 1983.

Ceiling

A plain ceiling with dentilled cornicing.

Fireplace

Another Methley Hall fireplace with modern slips, grate and 18th century fire-irons.

Woodwork

A carved overdoor similar to that seen in the daughter's room and having a delicate double flowering rose at the centre. The architrave and skirting have matching pattern repeats whilst the surviving pieces of the dado on the east wall show a simple egg and dart pattern.

Paintings

Manner of Franc Francken (1581-1642). Flemish c.1630. The seven acts of mercy.
Flemish School (16th century). St. Francis of Assisi.
School of Thomas Gainsborough (1727-1788). Fishing from the shoreline.
South German School (16th century). St. Catherine of Alexandria and the conversion of the philosophers.
School of Richard Wilson (1713-1782). Arcadia.

Furniture

Commode Cupboard, mahogany, c.1765, with canted corners, serpentine front and fretwork in the Chinese taste.
Dressing Bureau, walnut, c.1715. A multi purpose piece of furniture intended to stand in a pier between windows.
Chair, one of six throughout the house, mahogany, c.1785 with wheatsheaf splat.
Sofa Table, rosewood, c.1820.
Secretaire, mahogany, c.1760, attributed to the workshops of William Vile. Pierced latticework superstructure and finely carved mouldings with a fall front writing board supported on brass quadrant brackets. The legs are chamfered on the inside and carved with trailing pendants of flowers.
Chair, one of two, walnut, c.1720, having drop-in seats upholstered in contemporary needlework showing scenes which seem to depict the various stages of courtship.
Table, mahogany, c.1825. Combined reading and writing table. Central pedestal and four reeded legs.
Press, mahogany, c.1750. The fielded door panels enclose a series of sliding trays used for the storage of clothes.
Chest of Drawers, walnut, c.1705, popularly referred to as a Bachelor's Chest.

Bed, mahogany with painted pine tester. Hung in a French 'Persepolis' pattern chintz. Design by Francis Johnson.

Clock

Bracket Clock, c,1700, 8-day, by Daniel Quare of London (1648-1724). a 6½ inch square dial with exposed arbors in the spandrels. The unusual case is possibly later.

Textiles

Quashgai rug, 19th century. A pale blue field with three lined pole medallions set in a dark brown border with yellow and ivory stripes.
Caucasian carpet. Broad red field in the style of the Bokhara. Modern.
Caucasian carpet. Pale blue and ivory in the style of a Yomud Bokhara. Modern.
Dressing gown, French, c.1800, embroidered silk with velvet cuffs and collar.

Ceramics

Part Wash Set, Mintons *Geneve* pattern, 19th century. ex: Harewood House.
Plate. An open scroll tells the story of a clandestine meeting between children on a terrace, in famille rose colours, Qianlong (1736-1795).
Plate, Imari pattern with peonies and chrysanthemums.
Plate, decorated in Imari colours.
Teapot, with reeded body and lid decorated in Imari colours.
Flared bowl, in famille verte colours painted with panels of sacred objects, Kangxi.

Miscellanea

Candlestick, brass, c.1800, with its original candle snuffer.
Cross, walnut, c.1690. Christ attended by robed figure. The reverse contains holy relics.
Cross, oak and ivory, c.1770 in the Jensenist manner showing a skull and crossbones symbolising Christ's death at Calvary.
Gabbrie Chiabrera, *Poesie liriche,* London, 1781.
Spectacles, iron and glass, late 18th century.
Rosary, c.1900, souvenir of Lourdes.
Wig Block, lime, late 18th century.
Reliquaries, c.1730, gilded pine frames with silk panels embroidered with silk and gold and representing S. Ignatius of Loyola and the Virgin Mary.
Bronze Bust, Menelaus, King of Sparta.

Exit through a jib door into the next room.

Drawing Room

Ceiling

An elaborate coffered coving which radiates towards the centre and focuses on an oval medallion of Amicitia, who is intended to represent Friendship. The Latin mottoes on the hem of her skirt, on ribbons in her hand and in the tree proclaim that friendship will survive all trials and tribulations, whilst the vine entwined round the elm tree testifies to the bond of brotherly love.

Surrounding this oval panel is an elaborate framework of swirling palm leaves and interlinking foliage.

Walls

Hung in a green cotton damask using a popular 18th century 'Artichoke' pattern. The room had formed part of the 20th century dancehall and restoration involved the creation of the jib door and replacement of the connecting wall between this and the Saloon.

Fireplace

A replacement fireplace in the neo-classical style with white statuary and crossbanded Connemara marble c.1775, that probably came from Powerscourt House, Dublin. The steel grate and the serpentine-fronted fender with its pierced Anthemion pattern are contemporary with the fireplace, as are the brass handled fire-irons.

Paintings

William Etty (1787-1849). Figure of a seated man.

William Etty. Back view of a nude woman leaning against a draped pedestal.

William Etty. S.A. Baynton, M.P. York 1830-32.

William Etty. Nude woman full length, holding red drapery.

William Etty. Figures in an arcadian landscape.

Artist unknown. Portrait of a lady in yellow satin dress.

T. Ramos (1989). Charles Gregory 9th Viscount Fairfax of Emley.

Artist unknown, c.1720. Portrait of a gentleman in blue. The stretcher is signed John Tregeagle Esq.

Maria Verelst, (1680-1740). English c. 1740. Portrait of a lady in blue.

Philip Mercier (1689-1760). Lady Mary Fairfax, signed and dated 1741.

Studio of Sir Joshua Reynolds (1723-1792). Mary Palmer, Marchioness of Thomond.

Furniture

Cabinet, Kingwood, c.1690, oyster-cut veneering.

Cabinet on Stand, seaweed marquetry, c.1695. ex: Cora, Countess of Strafford.

Quartetto Tables, amboyna, c.1790.

Torchère, one of two, mahogany, c.1760. Carved in the Chinese style.

Armchair, mahogany and velvet, c.1735. Bold cabriole legs and hairy paw feet.

Games Table, sabicu, c.1800, for chess and backgammon.

Stool, walnut, c.1720, parcel-gilt cabriole legs and gros-point needlework.

Cabinet on Stand, walnut, fruitwoods, ivory, c.1700. The fall front reveals 48 drawers, 21 of which are 'secret'.

Chair, mahogany, c.1780. Popularly referred to as in the Hepplewhite style.

Card Table, mahogany, c.1765. Attributed to the workshop of Joseph Ward, London. Geometric marquetry top and cabriole legs.

Writing Table, walnut, c.1690. Central legs pivot out to support hinged top.

Torchère, mahogany, c.1760. Fretted gallery in Gothic taste.

Chair, one of two, walnut, c.1720. Contemporary needlework seats portraying various stages of courtship.

Bureau Bookcase, walnut, c.1700. Fitted out with drawers, compartments and Corinthian columns that support Roman figures.

Clocks

Bracket Clock, c.1720, No.753 by George Graham of London (1673-1751). An 8-day movement with a verge escapement and pull quarter repeat, set in veneered ebony case.

Longcase Clock, c.1700 by Daniel Quare of London (1648-1724). An 11 inch square dial set in a veneered walnut case.

Textiles

Tekke Bokhara, Turkoman c.1850.

Tekke Bokhara, Turkoman c.1900. Three columns of octagons divided by ghuls.

Hatchli Engsi (prayer rug). Yomud region of Turkestan, c.1900. Broad X and Y motifs within a stylised floral vine border.

Metalwork

Candlesticks, Sheffield plated, telescopic.

Ceramics

Various bowls and vases painted in famille verte colours illustrating Chinese figures, antiquities, flowers, birds and mythical beasts, all Kangxi (1662-1722).

Enter the Saloon through the restored doorcase.

Saloon

This room formed the main part of the dancehall from 1920 to 1982 and had been used as a billet for the armed forces during World War II. Fortunately the soldiers were reasonably careful. Beams had been inserted by the cinema company to support the ceilings and reinstatement was therefore confined to the east and west walls, floor and fireplace.

Ceiling

Perhaps the most accomplished and naturalistic of all the ceilings in the house with the swirling movement of its vine entwined central ellipse and ceiling rose. Medallions of musical instruments and an open manuscript showing the 18th century ballad of 'Belinda and Amelia', all set in oak leaf garlands, proclaim the room's intended use and the scrolling strapwork supports baskets of fruit and flowers in representation of the seasons. The whole is supported by an unusual dentilled cornice of spouting lions whilst below, a flowing frieze of raffle leaf and flower completes the scheme.

Walls

Covered in a crimson cotton damask in accord with the decoration of 1762.

Woodwork

Although the original fireplace had been removed, the two doorcases on the north wall had remained and these provided the pattern for the replacement on the east elevation.

The pulvinated friezes have like many in the house a rose at their centre and the entablature above is carved to match the designs on the ceiling cornice.

Window architraves have 'eared' mouldings of shell, flower and egg similar to that in the Dining room whilst dado and skirting are carved with foliage and fan.

The only surviving mahogany door is to the left of the fireplace, a dummy door introduced, like that on the great staircase landing, to give balance to the room.

Fireplace

A replacement of Siena and statuary marble with Ionic columns that support a frieze decorated with a Greek key pattern and a centre tablet of fruit and flowers. Reputed to have come out of a house in Mayfair.

The attendant grate, pierced fender and brass handled fire-irons are contemporary with the chimneypiece.

Windows

In 1762 the Viscount replaced most of the sash windows with new oak ones and these have survived with only minor repair. The carved shutters are original and originally secured from within by means of a sliding bar.

Paintings

Artist unknown. Said to be a Portrait of 'Black Tom', General Thomas Fairfax c.1645.
Mason Chamberlain. (1730-1795). Portrait of a gentleman in red.
Attributed to Sir Godfrey Kneller (1649-1723). John Churchill, 1st Duke of Marlborough.
Manner of Willem Wissing (1656-1687). King James II. On loan from Castle Howard.
Mason Chamberlain. Portrait of gentleman.
Manner of Jean François de Troy (1679-1752). James Francis Edward Stuart, 'The Old Pretender'.
Dirck Maas (1656-1717). Hunting scene.
Artist unknown, c.1795. Miss Busby, later married to a Councillor Piggott, perhaps one of the Piggotts of Gilling Castle.
J.F. Nollekens (1702-1748). Lord Tylney and his family and friends at Wanstead House, Essex, signed and dated 1740.

Sir Thomas Lawrence (1769-1830). Louisa Jane Allen, c.1795. Married to John Wedgwood, eldest son of Josiah Wedgwood.
Dirck Maas. Hunting in a country park.
After Sir Peter Lely (1618-1680). King Charles II. On loan from Castle Howard.
Manner of D. Teniers, the Younger (1610-1694). Village scene.

Furniture

Chair, one of three, mahogany, c.1760. Excellent examples of where the rococo, Gothic and Chinese tastes are combined.
Square Piano, 1792, No.325 by Thomas Haxby, York (1729-1796). The third pedal operated the lid 'swell' by means of a piston.
Urn Stand, mahogany, c.1760. Decorated in the Gothic taste, supporting plated hot water urn c.1780.
Table, mahogany, c.1760. Lavishly carved legs and scrolled toes after designs by Ince and Mayhew.
Tea-caddy, burr-yew and bronze, c.1790. Sarcophagus shape and locking lid.
Sofa, mahogany, c.1785. Delicate cabriole legs and masked toes.
Tripod Table, one of two, mahogany. Theories abound as to their intended use. The very plainness of the tops would suggest that they supported a silver salver and that the recesses were intended to prevent the feet slipping off. They could then be used for a 'stirrup cup' and be found located in a large hall.
Tea Table, mahogany, c.1760. Probably Irish.
Armchair, mahogany, c.1760. After a design by Thomas Chippendale.
Armchair, one of two, mahogany, c.1760. Attributed to the workshop of John Gordon. The curved arms and inswept supports are carved with a double band of fishscaling and this imbrication is repeated on the shaped seat rails and cabriole legs. ex: Ditton Park.
Chest of Drawers, mahogany. After a design by Thomas Chippendale.
Chair, one of two, mahogany, c.1760. Closely related to a design by Thomas Chippendale in his *Director.*
Chest of Drawers, mahogany, c.1760. Distinctive bombé form, closely related to Chippendale's design for a *'French Commode'.* ex: Earl of Dartmouth.

Chest of Drawers, mahogany, c.1775, with serpentine front and fluted corners.
Card Table, one of two, mahogany, c.1765. Slender cabriole legs, one of which pivots out to support the hinged top. ex: Stevenson Hall.
Pier Glass, one of two, in the rococo style.
Chest of Drawers, mahogany, c.1760. Canted corners enriched with consoles of foliage. Splayed bracket feet in the Chinese taste.
Chandelier, brass c.1920 in Queen Anne style.

Clocks

Bracket Clock, c.1708, No.475 by Thomas Tompion and Edward Banger (partnership 1701-1708). 8-day movement with original crown wheel escapement. ex: Princess Louise, 4th daughter of Queen Victoria.
Longcase Clock, c.1695 by Joseph Windmills of London (fl.1671-1710). 12 inch square dial set in a walnut case decorated with arabesque designs in seaweed marquetry.

Ceramics

Kendi, painted with flowers and 'Persian' profiles in famille verte colours, Kangxi.
Bowl, one of two with shallow domed covers. Famille verte colours painted with birds, flowers and foliage, Kangxi.
Dish, painted with a dragon chasing a flaming pearl, in famille verte colours, Chenghua mark, Kangxi.
Standing Boy, holding vase of flowers, famille verte colours, Kangxi.
Vase, oviform with carved wooden cover and painted with Buddhisztic lions, Kangxi.
Bowl, panels of family figures in a garden setting. Famille rose colours, late Qianlong.
Dish, flowers and insects rising from a rock outcrop, Kangxi.
Rice Bowl, rim decorated with dragons that chase the flaming pearl whilst within, figures and scripts illustrate scenes from the *Po Ku.*
Soup Bowl, decorated in famille verte colours.
Plate, one of two, painted with storks on the rim and a stork and deer sheltering below a pine tree, all in famille verte colours, Kangxi.

Carpet

Wilton carpet woven with motifs at the centre and in the border. These were chosen to complement the decoration of the room.

Exit through the jib door into the exhibition room.

Fairfax House
The Owners

York in the 18th century had become the social centre for the northern gentry and aristocracy, whose fine town houses built in brick were springing up all over the city. There were several in Castlegate, such as Castlegate House, almost opposite Fairfax House, which we know was built to the designs of John Carr specifically for Peter Johnson, the Recorder of York. It was completed in 1763.[53]

The early history of Fairfax House is rather more obscure, although there is documentary evidence of three owners or occupiers prior to the Fairfaxes, the earliest recorded being Thomas Laycon Barker in 1744.[54] He had inherited the property from his uncle Thomas Barker of Otley and Castlegate, York, who was a barrister at law and a wealthy York citizen of some standing.[55]

From 1750 the house was owned by Joseph Marsh 'of Harrigate (sic), coal merchant, dealer and chapman.' He occupied it for 8 years before becoming a bankrupt in 1758. In the following year it was leased to 'Boynton Wood, Esq.' He was the elder son of John Wood, a barrister from an established Yorkshire family who in 1719 had purchased Hollin Hall, near Ripon, which is still the family home. He was related by marriage to another great Yorkshire family, the Boyntons.[56]

The first mention of Fairfax is to be found in the land tax register for Castlegate in 1760/1 and shows the rateable value: 'The Hon. Miss Fairfax's house and garden - £18.'

Charles Gregory, the 9th Viscount Fairfax of Emley in the Peerage of Ireland, and his only surviving daughter Anne, were the last of the senior line of

Artist unknown, c.1730. Charles Gregory, 9th Viscount Fairfax of Emley.

the Fairfaxes. The name, however, lives on today through other branches of the family and it is perhaps appropriate at this point to look at the family history in some detail in order to place the 9th Viscount in his proper context. An abridged version of the pedigree is shown at the front of this guide for more general use.

The name Fairfax derives from the Saxon word 'feax' meaning hair, and it is likely that the Viscount's fair-haired ancestors were well established in England by the time of the Norman conquest.[57]

However, it is not until the early 13th century that more reliable records become available and from that time forward the family tree grows and expands. Through all the complexities of the long pedigree it is possible to identify three main branches of the family. First, the senior line whose estate was originally at Walton near Wetherby, and later at Gilling Castle in the Howardian hills some twenty miles north of York.

From this senior line sprang the two most important branches, the Fairfaxes of Steeton near Tadcaster, and of Denton near Otley. As the family developed and prospered, so they acquired other manors in the process, mainly in Yorkshire, and usually within easy reach of York. It was therefore natural that they came to have strong associations with the city.[58]

In the year 1205, it is recorded that one Richard Fairfax possessed land at Askham near York. Little else is known about him, but it was not long before Fairfaxes began to take a prominent part in the affairs of Yorkshire. In 1249 Richard's grandson, William, was Bailiff of York and was clearly a wealthy and influential citizen. He it was who purchased the manor of Walton from Peter de Brus. Like so many of his successors he also had a town house in York, for in 1257 he was living in a stone mansion near Ouse Bridge. Only the wealthiest of York citizens could have afforded to import stone for building.

By 1492 the Gilling estate had come into Fairfax hands and in that year Sir Thomas Fairfax (one of at least 36 recorded Thomases), who was Master of the King's Horse, inherited Gilling Castle by descent as heir to his ancestor Sir Ivo de Etton. From that time on Gilling became pre-eminent as the

Gilling Castle, South front.

country seat of the senior line of the Fairfaxes and remained so until the line became extinct in 1793. This side of the family had staunchly maintained their Roman Catholic faith to the end.

Engraved by Daniel King, c.1655-60.

The Steeton branch of the family had its origins in the latter half of the 15th century. Sir Guy Fairfax was the third son of a Fairfax of Walton, a colourful character who had made his own way in the world. He was Recorder of York from 1460 to 1477 and then became a Judge of the King's Bench. In the process of his rise to power he had become Lord of the Manor of Steeton, where he built a house and a chapel, consecrated by Archbishop Neville in 1473. It is said that he always wore a white rose as a token of his affection and loyalty to the House of York. His immediate descendants had acquired several more Yorkshire manors; Bilbrough, Nun Appleton and Bolton Percy, all near York, and most importantly, Denton.

The Denton branch grew quickly and prospered, helped by judicious marriage settlements and also, no doubt, by transferring their allegiance to the Protestant faith in c.1575 soon after the Reformation. This branch produced the two greatest figures in the Fairfax dynasty. Ferdinando, 2nd Baron Fairfax of Cameron, was General of Cromwell's

Parliamentary forces from 1642 to 1645. He died in 1647 and was succeeded by his even more famous son Thomas, 'Black Tom', Commander-in-Chief of the New Model Army, whose dark complexion belied his ancestral name. Despite his military prowess, General Fairfax was modest and retiring by nature and liked nothing better than to retreat to his gardens and meadows at Nun Appleton in the company of his daughter and her accomplished tutor Andrew Marvell, arguably England's greatest poet.

He also built himself a fine town house in York and took great pride in the City. During the siege of York in 1644 strict instructions were issued to the Parliamentary forces that no damage was to be done to the Minster and it is largely due to General Thomas Fairfax and his father that York was spared the Puritan excesses of destruction which swept through England after the Civil War.

Thomas Fairfax's imposing mansion on Bishophill, which he gave to his daughter Mary on the occasion of her marriage to George Villiers, 2nd Duke of Buckingham, was a landmark in the city for several generations.[59] It has long since disappeared, but it is still commemorated in the names of Bishophill streets.

There soon followed a remarkable expansion of the Denton Fairfaxes to America. The 5th Lord Fairfax of Cameron had married into the Culpeper family, to whom a grateful Charles II had given vast tracts of land in the new colony of Virginia as a reward for his active support at the time of the Restoration. When financial difficulties eventually forced the sale of all their Yorkshire estates, including those at Denton, the impoverished heir emigrated to America to claim and protect the Culpeper inheritance. His descendants reaped the benefit from the rapidly increasing value of the 5 million acres of land, much of which now forms part of Greater Washington. The present name of Fairfax County, Virginia, is a reminder of its origins.

The Steeton Fairfaxes had never achieved quite the same status as the other two branches and were never elevated to the peerage. However, they too played a prominent part in local and national affairs. Throughout their history, Fairfaxes have always felt a compulsive attraction towards service in the armed forces. The two famous civil war generals were far from being the only Fairfaxes to give valiant service in the army. Indeed, General Thomas' brother, Charles, was slain at the battle of Marston Moor. The navy too was the chosen career of many members of the family, and probably the most eminent of the seafaring Fairfaxes was Admiral Robert, one time Lord of the Admiralty.

Robert Fairfax of Steeton was born in 1665 and entered the navy as a young

Sir Thomas Fairfax. Engraved by Houbraken after a painting by Cooper.

Artist unknown, Admiral Robert Fairfax c.1695. On loan from York City Art Gallery.

man, obtaining at the age of 25 his first command.[60] During his long and distinguished career he took part in many daring actions at sea, eventually serving on the Council of Admiralty. After retiring from the navy he occupied himself with more local affairs, becoming Lord Mayor of York in 1715. He also represented York for two years as one of its Members of Parliament. His York residence was at 71 Micklegate, and during his later years he busied himself in moving the family home from Steeton to Newton Kyme where 'he built himself a pleasant seat in 1714 and planted a fine avenue of trees'.[58]

Returning now to the Fairfaxes of Gilling; they had for some time been very much pre-occupied with their own affairs in Yorkshire and had skilfully managed to avoid the severest penalties of recusancy.[61]

Nevertheless, by the early 17th century both the Denton and the Gilling branches of the Fairfaxes had become prominent in aristocratic society. There would no doubt have been some consternation at Gilling when Sir Thomas Fairfax of Denton was the first to be elevated to the peerage as the Baron Cameron in 1627. Thankfully the efforts of Sir Thomas of Gilling were soon rewarded when in 1628 he was created 1st Viscount Fairfax of Emley in the County of Tipperary, Ireland. The amount of £900 which he had to pay for the honour probably seemed worthwhile.

The next 110 years saw the rather rapid passing of eight Viscounts Emley, and it was in 1738 that Charles Gregory Fairfax succeeded to the title.[62]

Charles Gregory's exact year of birth is unknown, but it must have been around 1700. He was educated at Lambspring College in Austria. His father, who served abroad as an officer in the Imperial Army, had succeeded to the title very unexpectedly in 1719, after the premature demise of no fewer than 20 more eligible heirs in the entail. Indeed, the impoverished Denton Fairfaxes had had their hopes raised high. Henry Culpeper Fairfax wrote to his brother the 6th Baron Fairfax of Cameron on 15th October 1715 'I hear the Lord Fairfax of Gilling is very weak and if he dies Walton and other Mannours will fall to you as next Protestant heir.' But in the event they did not and, as we have seen, the disappointed 6th Baron eventually emigrated to America.

Up to 1719 Charles Gregory had lived abroad in somewhat straitened circumstances like his father, apparently having difficulty in finding employment. When the family returned to England in that year, new horizons were opened up and visits to London society became frequent. His newly formed aristocratic connections soon bore fruit and in 1720 he married Elizabeth, the widow of the 4th Viscount Dunbar of Burton Constable. This union was a great help in stabilising the estate's precarious finances.

Any happiness resulting from this marriage was short-lived. In April 1721, whilst on a visit to Bath to take the waters, Elizabeth contracted smallpox and died. A year later, in May 1722, Charles married again, this time to a distant cousin Mary Fairfax, to whom he became deeply devoted. It was an extremely fruitful union, producing nine children in little more than a decade. By 1736 he had two daughters and three sons still living and the family succession seemed secured, but disaster soon struck again. By 1739 Fairfax had lost his second wife and all his remaining children in smallpox epidemics, except for two daughters, Anne and Elizabeth. All his hopes and ambitions had been

P. Mercier (1689-1760). The two Miss Fairfaxes, signed and dated 1742.

mercilessly extinguished, and his outlook and way of life profoundly changed. The final blow came in 1753 when Elizabeth was also taken from him by smallpox, leaving the melancholy Anne and her grieving father to face the future alone.

Although he took a proprietorial interest in his country estate at Gilling, Lord Fairfax was essentially a townsman by nature. After the family tragedies of the 1730s he spent much of his time in London, first in a variety of lodgings and then as a paying guest in the houses of his Bredall and Piggott relations. Fairfax had always taken a dutiful interest in the upbringing of his nephews, but Francis Bredall, in particular, turned out to be a somewhat odious character. It is likely that Fairfax had paid for his education at Lambspring and had also financed his apprenticeship to a York apothecary before 1736. In return for this characteristic generosity, Francis Bredall pestered the Viscount incessantly for money and no member of the Fairfax establishment, human or otherwise, was allowed to escape the benefits of his rudimentary medical training. His lengthy and frequent apothecary's bills include such items as:-

	s	d
The stomatick tincture Yr Lordship	2	6
Purging potion with manna for Miss	1	0
A detergent gargle, Laundry Maid	1	0
Horse balls	7	6

Judging from this example, the veterinary side of the business seems to have been the more profitable.[63]

While in London, Fairfax moved mainly in Catholic circles and had few Protestant friends. For his infrequent visits to York during this period he rented houses in the City.

Occasionally while in Yorkshire, the family would visit Harrogate and Knaresborough to take the waters, perhaps avoiding Bath because of the sad

Moses Griffiths, Harrowgate Wells (sic), signed and dated 1772.

memories it held for him. They may have had good Catholic reasons for going to Harrogate however, for Celia Fiennes on her journey in 1697 noted that a Spring 'St. Mongers (Mungo) Well' at Copgrove (near Harrogate) was popular with Papists. She recounts the story that a new born infant had once been abandoned in the parish and was brought up by the church wardens. When the child grew up he 'attained learning and was a very religious man and used the well to wash himself'. The many cures which he achieved resulted in the well retaining its attractions for the sick long after his death.

Celia Fiennes took a more down to earth view: 'Setting aside the Papists fancyes of it, I cannot but think it is a very good Spring, being remarkably cold, and just at the head of the Spring so its fresh which must needs be very strengthening, it shuts up the pores of the body immediately so fortifyes from cold, you cannot bear the coldness of it above 2 or 3 minutes... You go in and out in Linnen Garments, some go in flannell, I used my Bath garments... but some will keep on their wet garments and let them drye to them and say its more beneficial, but I did not venture it... Some of the Papists I saw there had so much Zeale as to continue a quarter of an hour on their knees at their prayers in the Well, but none else could well endure it so long a time.'[64]

We may be reasonably sure that Lord Fairfax took care not to become involved in the 'troublesome delight' encountered by Thomas Baskerville when he had journeyed to Knaresborough Spa in 1675. '.....an importunity among the women (as to) who shall be your servant to fill water for you..... one cries out 'I am pretty Betty, let me serve you;' another cries 'Kate and Coz Dol, do let we serve you', but to tell the truth they fell short of that for their faces did shine like bacon rine. And for beauty may vie with an old Bath guide's ass, the sulphur waters had so fouled their pristine complexion'.[65]

According to one of his relations, Lord Fairfax was said to be both obstinate and scrupulous and this shrewd judgement of his character shows through in many of his dealings. We have seen how he felt it his duty to look after the welfare of his nephews. He got himself entangled to an even greater extent in the affairs of the Gascoignes of Parlington, to whom he was related by marriage. At first he managed to extricate himself quite neatly. When an attempt was made in 1749 to make him an executor in the affairs of Sir Edward Gascoigne his brother-in-law, he wrote to Gascoigne, 'I had a letter from the great Duchess our cosen, if I dare call her so. I may venture to say I shall never have another.' The 'Duchess' was a distant relation, the formidable Mary, widow of the 8th Duke of Norfolk. She was wealthy, childless and notoriously difficult to cope with.

But Sir Edward died in the following year and inevitably Fairfax had to become his executor and co-guardian of the two sons, Sir Edward and Thomas Gascoigne. They proved to be more than a handful for him. The boys were sent to school at Douai, and despite reassurances from France, Fairfax was in a constant state of alarm over rumours of their activities, which included some dancing parties and a visit to Cambrai where Sir Edward was said to have given a ball for the school girls there; it was all no doubt greatly exaggerated though subsequent events were to confirm the Viscount's fears. When the young Sir Edward died suddenly of smallpox in 1762, quarrels among the guardians resulted in a costly and acrimonious law-suit in Chancery.

F. Hayman (1708-1776), The Gascoigne Family, c.1745.

This was by no means the only lawsuit in which Fairfax became involved during the course of his life. Nor was it the end of his troubles with the Gascoigne boys. Thomas proved to be a wilful and capricious youth who rebelled against the severe discipline of the monastic style of life at Douai, and was lured by the temptations of Paris and Italy. Eventually the worst happened. After a visit to Rome, where he became involved in a brawl, Thomas returned to England and apostasised. No wonder that Lord Fairfax took a gloomy view of the future of catholicism in England.

In following the strong Catholic tradition of the Gilling line, Fairfax found himself in trouble from time to time. He had refused to take the oath of allegiance in 1745, at the time of the Jacobite troubles when the authorities were particularly jittery. The then Archbishop of York, Thomas Herring, had already had occasion to warn Lord Fairfax that he was to be more circumspect in the practice of his religion, and in September 1745 Herring wrote to the Secretary of State, Lord Hardwicke, 'Lord Falconbridge (sic) dined with me yesterday... he offered a sort of security for the honour and innocence of his relation and neighbour Lord Fairfax of Gilling, and intimated to lodge a deposition with me. I told him that was a matter of some nicety but whatever I saw in favour of Lord Fairfax, notwithstanding my good opinion of him, must rest upon his authority.'

Consequently, there was considerable alarm in York when the rumour spread that Fairfax was harbouring troops at Gilling Castle in readiness for an uprising. The Rector of Gilling, Nicholas Gouge, wrote to Lord Irwin, the Lord Lieutenant, on October 1st — 'Yesterday Lord Fairfax sent down his coachman who is a Protestant to me with compliments, and to acquaint me that one of our Town, his Lordship's tenant too, a most bigotted Papist had given out that there was a private room within Gilling Castle where 40 men might be conceal'd and nobody cou'd find them out and his Lordship desir'd the person might be brought before me and punish'd as the law directs: and further his Lordship desir'd that I would send the Constable. . . to search his castle whether there was any such room or not . . . (the searchers went there and) saw the place at the end of the Ale Cellar . . . not two yards square . . . The Lord's Coachman assured me that of late there had been no company excepting Mr. Cholmondley and his wife.'

The story proved to be nothing more than the malicious gossip of a disaffected

T. Hudson (1701-1779), Thomas Herring, Archbishop of York (1743-1747), signed and dated 1743.

servant. Calm was restored and the incident ended on a companionable note. Archbishop Herring wrote afterwards, 'I believe Mr. Frankland and myself took the thing too high. . .but the recorder was frightened and the fright caught the city. . .Lord Fairfax was pleased with the opportunity of justifying himself. He treated Mr. Dunbar (the officer who went with the search warrant) at dinner and drank King George's health.'

Clearly, the Viscount was not prepared to put his family and estates at risk over his religion. However it is recorded[62] that he had in his possession an engraved Jacobite glass c.1735.

Despite his deep religious convictions and his pessimistic belief that Catholicism in England was doomed to extinction, Fairfax was a patriotic supporter of king and country, regularly subscribing to several newspapers and political publications, including Parliamentary debates in the House of Commons. Other book purchases include such diverse items as The Letters of Fabricius ab Aquapendente, the great 16th century Italian anatomist, and the works of Rousseau (Fairfax could speak French fluently).

That he was also interested in the scientific advances of the age and in the arts, is evident from the busts of Newton and Shakespeare on the staircase walls of Fairfax House and it is interesting that in correspondence with his ward, Sir Edward Gascoigne, he counselled the boy on the advantages of studying the theories of Newton whilst in France.

Apart from his religion, Lord Fairfax's greatest enthusiasm was for building and interior decoration. During the 1730s and 40s he had completely transformed the appearance of Gilling Castle, which occupies an impressive position on a hill above the village and church some 20 miles north of York.

Gilling Castle, West front.

The then little-known Italian stuccoist, Joseph Cortese, was employed on some of the interiors and had completed his work on the long gallery by 1742.

Architecturally the gallery lacks conviction and has an uneasy feel to it, with its elongated columns and rather weak central arches, suggesting that Fairfax was his own architect in this instance. His use of the carved wooden medallions in the spandrels of the arches illustrating classical figures of ancient Rome was very much in keeping with the period and would have appealed to the writer and painter Jonathan Richardson who felt rather pompously that 'no nation under Heaven so nearly resembles the ancient Greeks and Romans than we. There is a haughty courage, an elevation of thought, a greatness of taste, a love of liberty, a simplicity, an honesty amongst us, which we inherit from our ancestors and which belongs to us as Englishmen'.

The original core of the building is mediaeval, going back to the time of the Ettons in the 14th century, but successive generations of Fairfaxes had already made substantial changes by the 18th century, their most impressive contribution being the beautiful Tudor Great Chamber of c.1580. The 9th Viscount however, re-orientated the house, creating a new front entrance in the classical style, with projecting side wings.

After a spell in London, Lord Fairfax returned to live in Yorkshire in the late 1750s and by now he had decided to

The West end of the Long Gallery.

The East end.

The White Ante-room.

had not seen him before it was at an end it might have give one now and then some uneasiness thinking I had been to hasty, and I have the satisfaction that your God daughter is now more chearfull than ever I knew altho I have said nothing to her, by which as Mrs Forcer tells me, she does not doubt it is at an end. I bless God for her perseverance as I think there could not have been much happyness for her to have been expected . . .'

The events of 1755 however must have been even more traumatic for Anne. She had become engaged to William Constable of Burton Constable. This was to have been the third inter-marriage between the two families and it would have meant the absorption of the Fairfax estates into the far larger Constable properties. Later, in the next generation, as usually happened in such cases, a younger son of the marriage would have changed his name to Fairfax and resumed the estates.

The trousseau was bought in London. A special licence was procured in May 1755 and both families converged on London for the wedding in mid-June. Fairfax, however, was suspicious of the faith of the younger generation of English Catholics and from early in the affair Constable had had to give verbal assurances that he would go to the sacraments and practise his religion faithfully. But suspicion of him in the minds of Fairfax and his daughter remained although, according to Fairfax, they breathed no word to others. Not long before the date of the marriage, in a letter to Anne, Constable happened to mention that 'he had only been to prayers on two working days.' This seemed to mean that he hardly ever went to Mass on weekdays. Fairfax at once began to wonder whether this meant that his attendance at Mass on days of obligation was irregular. He considered it his duty

devote himself wholeheartedly to caring for his only surviving daughter Anne. The Viscount's influence on his daughter must have been considerable. He had been the instigator of some very serious disappointments and this would no doubt have soured her outlook on life.

Among the many aristocratic visitors to Gilling Castle during the 1740s was Thomas Clifton of Lytham, who seems to have formed an attachment to Anne. In 1749 a match was proposed, but this did not meet with Lord Fairfax's approval and the matter was not allowed to proceed further. He wrote to Sir Edward Gascoigne on 22nd April 1749 – 'I would not omit to let me dear Bart. know immediately that I have had the great Esq. of Lytham a week at Gilling. I am glad I know him. I cane but say that if I

Henry Walton (1720-1790), William Constable, c.1750.

to mention his doubts to his daughter. She at once wrote to her fiancé to demand in writing a solemn promise that he would practise his religion. When no satisfactory answer came, Lord Fairfax weighed in with a short and highly emotional note. Anne returned her ring to her fiancé and, after last minute and bungled efforts to see Constable, Fairfax took her home to Gilling.

It was not long after these traumatic events that Fairfax conceived the idea of building a fine new town house for her in York. Tradition has it that he spent £30,000 on the property he acquired in Castlegate, but £10,000 is more likely and even this was a huge sum in those days. He had a more specific purpose in mind for the property than most of his fellow noblemen who were embarking on similar projects. His Lordship fervently hoped that the house would be the means by which his lonely and neurotic daughter would be able to meet people and find a suitable partner.

If Lord Fairfax had hoped that Anne would recover her lost spirits, he was to be sadly disappointed and it is hardly surprising, after the tragic experiences of her earlier years and the unsettling circumstances of these recent abortive engagements, that she suffered from acute nervous disorders. In the hope of effecting some kind of cure, her father arranged for her to visit France under the care of his chaplain, Fr. Anselm Bolton. She went into Retreat at Cambrai and then on to the English Benedictine convent in Brussels, but all to no avail and eventually she returned home, her health in no way improved.

The Viscount's costly building ventures, combined with a certain lack of discipline in controlling his business affairs, began to cause him increasing financial embarrassment. 'My daughter's house, which is just finished and paid for, drains me of all my money', he writes plaintively to his London banker in 1762. However, long before this, his financial problems had led him to sell most of his Yorkshire estates including Walton, Scawton, West Heslerton, Acaster and Coulton. The sales brought him in some £50,000, but at the cost of reducing his annual income from rents from just over £2,000 to about £750. After paying off debts against the estate he was left with about £20,000 and invested his lump sums in an odd variety of undertakings, the most remarkable being the purchase of no less than £11,000 worth of shares in the cargo of the ship 'Amable Maria' operated by Ryan and Mannock of Cadiz and sailing from Cadiz to Lima. This speculative venture was bitterly regretted by Fairfax and the late arrival of the ship on the homeward journey was the cause of many a sleepless night. He also had interests in Thomas Mannock's wine importing business and bought shares in Dormer & Fanning, assurance brokers in

Antwerp as an endowment for his daughter.

All these ventures were scarcely sufficient to enable him to keep a healthy bank balance, and he supplemented his income by steadily increasing the rents on his remaining estates and by selling off the timber from some of the woodlands.

As might be expected from his social position and strong religious convictions, Fairfax was deeply involved in the affairs of the Roman Catholic church. This often added to his problems, although he managed to extricate himself to some extent from many of the more onerous financial burdens. However, his obstinate character led to clashes of another kind. It was his practice to employ his own personal chaplain who would be expected to accompany him wherever he went, particularly on his journeyings from Gilling to York or London. Indeed, the chapel which he had incorporated in his Castlegate house must have been an elaborate affair, judging from the surviving bills for furnishing and for equipping it. Unfortunately, no trace of this chapel remains although Francis Johnson suggests that the long gallery formed by Lord Fairfax on the 2nd floor may have had this function. It was originally two rooms with a passage between. As a long gallery its function was completely out of date unless it had been on the *piano nobile* with the other main rooms.

The Viscount's standards were evidently very exacting, for he had secured the summary dismissal of at least seven chaplains with whom he had violently disagreed between 1750 and 1764. This high-handed attitude caused considerable friction between him and the Benedictine authorities, who felt that Fairfax was being most unreasonable. His main complaint was that young untrained priests were sent straight from their monasteries, without sufficient experience. However, though there seems to have been some truth in his allegation, the following letter from Fr. Jenkins, his chaplain at Gilling from 1761 to 1764, to Lord Fairfax in London, points to the main reason for the Viscount's displeasure.

'Holdens wife expressing great concern and apprehension lest her son should die without help, I thought it proper to acquaint your Lordship that I would stay at Gilling with your leave, till he is out of danger .... I am desired likewise to go to Rivies Abbey .... and to Hambleton..... If I may be allowed to give advice, twould be better for yr Lordship to miss prayers now and then on a Sunday rather than deprive many poor people of the assistance they seem gladly to stand in need of. Hoping yr Lordship will excuse the freedom I take in delivering my opinion.....'

Predictably, Father Jenkins was immediately dismissed, having held his position for three years. He was followed in 1764 by Fr. Anselm Bolton who proved to be more to the Viscount's liking, remaining with Fairfax for the rest of the Viscount's life and continuing as chaplain and mentor to Anne Fairfax at Gilling until her death in 1793.

The house in Castlegate was only occupied by the Fairfaxes for eleven brief winters. When her father died in 1772, Anne sold the house and within a year she had returned to Gilling Castle. Here she lived on, alone and emotionally disturbed, for another 21 years. When she died in 1793 at the age of about 68, the estate passed to her distant relative, Charles Gregory Piggott. He changed his name to Fairfax, and thus the name was perpetuated at Gilling for about another 100 years.

From Lord Fairfax's death in 1772 to 1865, his house in Castlegate changed hands six times.

From 1773 to 1780 it became the property of Mrs. Mary Thornton, widowed mother of the celebrated sportsman Colonel Thomas Thornton of Allerton Mauleverer, who had purchased the Allerton estate from the Duke of York in 1789 and ostentatiously renamed it Thornville Royal. He also owned the York Waterworks at Lendal Tower and added a lucrative supplement to his large inherited fortune by providing York citizens with a piped water supply.

The colonel was noted for his eccentric behaviour, exceeded only by that of his captivating 22-year old female companion, Alicia Meynell, who caused many a raised eyebrow when she took to horse racing under the name of Thornton. She it was who, in 1804, challenged a certain Captain Flint to a

Artist unknown, Alicia Meynell (called Mrs Thornton) c.1805.

John Russell (1745-1806), Portrait of Colonel Thomas Thornton. From the Halifax Collection.

four mile match on the Knavesmire for 1,000 guineas, an unheard of intrusion into the exclusively male world of horse racing. The contest naturally attracted enormous interest and excitement and on the day, Alicia quickly proved her superior horsemanship, taking the lead for most of the race. She lost only because of her horse going lame, but when Thornton refused to honour his debt, matters became acrimonious. The subsequent scandalous events built up to a climax the following year and culminated in Colonel Thornton being publicly horse-whipped by Flint because of his refusal to pay the 1,000 guineas. It became a *cause célèbre* of the day.[66] Mercifully, perhaps, old Mrs Thornton was by this time dead and no doubt able to take a more detached view of her son's disreputable conduct. Colonel Thornton erected a funeral monument to his mother in Allerton Park church.

Fairfax House was sold in 1780 to Walter Vavasour, who lived in it for seven years. He was a relation of the ancient Yorkshire family of Vavasour, whose ancestors had been Lords of Hazlewood Castle, Tadcaster, since the early 12th century and who in 1225 had granted to York Minster the freedom to use the stone from their quarries near Tadcaster. It was, indeed, a family into which an occasional Fairfax daughter had married.[67]

From 1787 to 1792 the house was owned by William Danby. He was descended from an old North Riding family and succeeded to his father's estates in 1781, when he became Lord of Mashamshire. An accomplished scholar and the author of several books, he was elected High Sheriff of Yorkshire in 1784. His country estate was at Swinton Park, Masham, where he carried out substantial improvements during his later life.[68]

For 28 years from 1792 the house belonged to one Peregrine Wentworth, who is recorded as becoming a bankrupt in 1820.

In 1820 the house was purchased by Sir John Lister-Kaye, whose family had a distinguished record of service to the city. His ancestor Sir John Lister Kaye was M.P. for York in 1734 and Lord Mayor in 1737 and the family coat of Arms appears on the outer face of Micklegate Bar, in commemoration of the Bar's restoration in 1737.[69]

The next owner, from 1840 to 1863, was Mrs Ann Mary Pemberton, widow of Ralph Stephen Pemberton of Barnes, County Durham. She was the daughter and heiress of Thomas Rippon, Esq. and niece of the Hon. Richard Hetherington, President of Tortola and the Virgin Islands.[70] The advertisement for the sale of the Castlegate residence which appeared in the Yorkshire Gazette in

RESIDENCE IN YORK.
TO BE SOLD BY PRIVATE CONTRACT,
(Or LET for a Term of Years,)

THE capital MANSION, situate in CASTLE-GATE, in the City of York, recently occupied by Mrs. PEMBERTON, deceased, containing on the ground Floor, Library and Dining Room; on the first floor, Two Drawing-Rooms, Ante-Room, One Bed-Room, and a Dressing-Room; on the second floor, Five Bed-Rooms, and Two Dressing-Rooms; also Two Kitchens, Servants' Hall, Housekeeper's Room and Pantries, with Servants' Apartments above. There are Three Coach-Houses and Stabling, for Nine Horses, Groom's House, Harness Room, Wash-House, and Laundry.
Immediate Possession can be given.
For further Particulars apply to Mr. MILLS, 3, Lendal, York.

Yorkshire Gazette, 19th September, 1863.

1863 gives an interesting description of Fairfax House as it existed at that time.

From 1865, after the death of Ann Pemberton, the house ceased to be a family home and over the next 100 years underwent a variety of changes in use from which its ultimate rescue and survival is little short of miraculous. It first became the office and meeting place of York Friendly Societies, many of which were springing up in the city to help the poorer element of the rapidly expanding Victorian population. These societies initially transacted their business in back street premises and public house parlours but soon found it necessary to obtain more suitable permanent accommodation. By 1885, part of Fairfax House was also being used as the office of the Ebor Permanent Benefit Building Society and this continued for about a quarter of a century.[71]

In 1876 the York City Club was founded, and Fairfax House took on a further burden of responsibility. The York Directory for 1909 includes the following entries for the house, No.27 Castlegate:-

Ebor Permanent Building Society
City Club
Hill, Henry T., Secretary,
Friendly Societies' Hall Co. Ltd.
Friendly Societies' Hall.

The most dramatic change of all, and potentially the most disastrous, came in 1919 when the first moves were made to convert the house into a cinema. Its preservation from much more serious damage, or perhaps total destruction, is probably due to the efforts of Dr. W.A. Evelyn, an early 20th century pioneer of conservation in York, who was able to obtain a grudging undertaking from the cinema company that they would endeavour to respect the architectural integrity of the house. The 1919 Conveyance records that the house and adjoining property to the left was sold to St. George's Hall Entertainments (York) Co. Ltd., for the sum of £6,995.[72]

Fairfax House as part of a Cinema, c.1925.

Fortunately the cinema was built at the side and rear of Fairfax House. The house itself was used for administrative purposes and for the other activities of this 'Entertainments' Company, the first floor rooms at the front being converted into a ballroom. The ballroom itself was put to a variety of uses during the 40 years of its existence. In 1934, for example, meetings of the Elim Four Square Gospel Alliance were held there before they moved to Swinegate and built the Elim Tabernacle.[73]

During the Second World War the armed forces were billeted there, to the consternation of the York Georgian Society. Their presence prompted the Society's Chairman, Oliver Sheldon, to write and ask that the men '. . . . . will be encouraged to preserve from damage the very elegant features of this old house.'[74]

In the early 1960s the Cinema Company decided to close St. George's Cinema and to dispose of their buildings in Castlegate. The City Council was approached, and decided to buy the whole site but primarily because of the special architectural qualities of Fairfax House. There was an inherited Dancing School tenancy, and so for over 20 years the Council was powerless to effect any proposals for Fairfax House, although it had been intended to use it as an annexe to the nearby Castle Museum. By the time the building became available the costs of undertaking the necessary restoration works were beyond the limited resources of the Council. In 1981 the offer made by the York Civic Trust to purchase from the Council and carry out comprehensive repairs to Fairfax House was accepted.

The Owners

c.1744	Thomas Laycon Barker
1750	Joseph Marsh ('of Harrigate')
1759	Boynton Wood (Leased)
1760	'The Hon. Miss Fairfax'
1773	Mrs Mary Thornton
1780	Walter Vavasour of Hazlewood
1787	William Danby, Esq., 'Lord of Mashamshire'
1792	Peregrine Wentworth
1820	Sir John Lister-Kaye
1840	Mrs Mary Ann Pemberton
1865	Use at various times by:- York Friendly Societies Ebor Building Society York City Club
1919	St. George's Hall Entertainments (York) Ltd. Cinema and Ballroom
1962	York City Council
1982	York Civic Trust

Noel Terry Collection

When the Trustees of the Noel G. Terry Charitable Trust decided to give Noel Terry's collection of furniture and clocks to the York Civic Trust, they were in fact fulfilling Noel Terry's often expressed wish.

He had originally desired that the collection should remain at his home, Goddards, and that the house be opened to the public, but he was wise enough not to tie the hands of his Trustees too tightly and he left the decision to them, with the proviso that whatever happened, the collection should stay as an entity in the City of York.[75]

Goddards, built for Noel Terry by Walter Brierley of York in 1926, gives the impression of being constructed for someone who liked early oak and walnut furniture. In the early '30s, Noel Terry did in fact buy some 17th-century pieces, including a finely carved buffet from William Randolph Hearst's collection, but he never seems to have shared that taste. The great strength of the collection is the mid-18th-century carved mahogany furniture, and it was obviously there that his real appreciation lay.

Noel Terry left a carefully worked out code (probably evolved late in the 1960s) of where and when he bought each piece and what he paid – and this allows a glimpse of the pattern of his buying and an appreciation of his developing taste and connoisseurship. As an extremely busy executive director of the family firm, it was difficult for him to create time to attend the great country house sales of the 1930s and 40s and he much preferred to place his trust in a few reputable dealers like Charles Thornton of York, Mallett's and latterly Hotspur, who were able to keep him in touch with current developments. By the 50s

Andrew Festing, 1985, Retrospective portrait of Noel Terry.

however, he was using Malletts as his agent in the salerooms of Christie's and Sotheby's although a serious illness in the 1960s reduced his mobility and he turned again to the advice of his trusted dealers.

His first purchase, still in the collection, is a lacquer low dresser bought in 1927 – the only piece of lacquer he appears to have bought – and this is now in the dining room at Fairfax House. In the years following the building of Goddards, most of his purchases, although always well chosen, seem to have been essentially for practical domestic use, but it is noticeable that they are almost all of a period later than that suggested by the house, giving the impression that he had developed a taste for the mid-18th-century quite early on.

Remarkably, he sustained his early enthusiasm as a collector for over half a century, and it is equally remarkable that his taste remained so consistent, both for what he liked and for what did not interest him. There is only one mirror in the collection, for instance, and that is the only example of the use of gilt or gilt-gesso. There is little later-18th-century furniture and even less of the Regency period, despite the fact that the Regency revival led by Edward Knoblock exercised such a powerful influence on taste in the 1920s. There was, perhaps, a puritanical and deliberately unfashionable streak in Noel Terry's character, which made him suspicious of the fashionable and the decorative.[76] He concentrated on the intrinsic quality and interest of individual pieces, with little concern for the relationship between pieces or between the furniture and its period setting.

It was just this singleminded concentration that enabled him to build up the collection over such a long time, and that gives the collection its strength. Gradually it became almost a sample collection, and has to be looked at in that way, as it brought together individual masterpieces, both major and minor, rather than balanced furnishings of a house. He was not interested in creating a period effect of any kind — albeit a 20th-century view of the 18th century. It was quite the opposite approach to Frank Green who, a generation earlier had created an eclectic mix of gilt, gilt-gesso, oak, walnut and mahogany for display in the Treasurer's House, York and it gives the Terry Collection a very distinct character. This is accentuated by the absence of any pieces with a strong architectural flavour, and by the predominance of the carver's rather than the designer's art.

It is not known whether Noel Terry was influenced by Frank Green but it is probably significant that between 1924 and 1927 the first edition of *The Dictionary of English Furniture* by Percy Macquoid and Ralph Edwards was published — building on the foundation of Macquoid's earlier *Age of Oak, Walnut, Mahogany* and *Satinwood*. Also in 1924, Oliver Brackett, a keeper at the V & A, published the first study of Chippendale's work and these volumes had formed the basis of Noel Terry's reference library.

Up to then, collectors such as Morgan S. Williams, Sir John Ramsden, Col. Norman Colville, and indeed Frank Green himself, had tended to concentrate on oak and early walnut, often combined with a strong interest in needlework. In the mid-'20s there was a slight shift in emphasis, and this period saw the formation of other celebrated collections of mid- and late-18th-century furniture, such as those of Leopold and Henry Hirsch, Colonel H. H. Mulliner and, particularly, Percival Griffiths and the 1st Viscount Leverhulme.

Noel Terry had much in common with these other collectors, like Percival Griffiths, who found it difficult to resist the acquisition of a rare or unusual piece. Whether a place could be found for it at home was, to them, a minor consideration and in later years, as furniture vans continued to turn up at 'Goddards' laden with another large piece of furniture, it was Mrs. Terry's practice to remind her husband about the lack of space left in the body of the house and to suggest that it would have to go into the attic.

Christie's have stated that Noel Terry created one of the best private collections of mid-18th century English furniture formed in the last fifty years. No mean praise, when we consider that it was put together during these halcyon years of the great country house sales and also when so many examples of this type of English furniture were being made available for collectors.

Mahogany Secretaire, c.1760 and walnut chair, c.1720.

Bracket clock, c.1700 by Daniel Quare.

Its display in Fairfax House however, has required several compromises in order that the integrity of both be maintained. A 20th century English gentleman's taste does not necessarily coincide with that of the 18th century Viscount for whom the house was built and it is unlikely that the house would have been arranged as we see it today.

Of the 154 pieces in the collection, 146 are on show to the general public and are distributed about the house in as logical a manner as possible, giving due consideration to the size and function of the pieces. It is unlikely that the Trust will add substantially to the assembly of furniture and clocks, but efforts will be made to improve the quality of the pictures and the silver on display.

The York Civic Trust gratefully acknowledge the generous sponsorship of Christie's in the production of a 152 page colour catalogue of the collection.

Copies may be obtained from York Civic Trust at a cost of £22 ($45) inc. of p. & p.

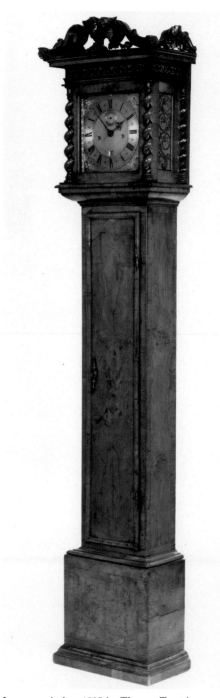

Longcase clock, c.1685 by Thomas Tompion.

References and Notes to the text

1. F. Drake, *Eboracum, A History of York,* 1735.

2. G. Webb, Y.A.Y.A.S. Times, No. 17, 1986, p.12.

3. N.C.R.O. ZDV(F), mic., 1132. Schedule of deeds & writings.

4. Borthwick Institute, PR Y/mic., 112. Land Tax Register for Castlegate.

5. ZDV(F).

6. York Courant, 14:7:1761. Notice of sale of some contents.

7. R. Davies, *A memoir of John Carr.* Yorkshire Archaeological Journal, Vol.4, 1877, pp. 202-213.

8. C.P. Curran, *Riverstown House, Co.Cork, and the Francini.* (copy with F. Johnson). Paul and Philip Francini were also responsible for the important Saloon ceiling at Bedale Hall, now council offices.

9. C.P. Curran, *Dublin Decorative Plasterwork,* 1967, p.28.

10. . . . ., Gilling Castle, Country Life, Sept.26, 1908, p.425. Heraldic panel above the fireplace in the Great Chamber.

11. Information provided by Dr. Ivan Hall.

12. Elizabeth Dove, *Sir Edward Gascoigne, Grand Tourist,* Leeds Art Calendar, Vol.2, 1976.

13. York Courant, 19:8:1793. 'Selling off at the warehouse of Messrs. Marshall & Sons in Petergate this week: A large quantity of Silver Plate and a valuable library, late property of the Hon. Miss Fairfax, Gilling Castle, 26:8:1793. Sale to continue until Wednesday next.'

14. *Joseph Addison,* perhaps modelled from a John Cheere bust, an example of which from the Kirkleatham collection is at York City Art Gallery. litt: M.I. Webb, Burlington Magazine, *Henry Cheere, Sculptor & Businessman,* Aug, 1958.
John Locke, there are two possible sources for this, both based on original images by Sir G. Kneller. The earliest, engraved by George Vertue in 1713 was extremely popular and is used on the frontispiece of *The Works of John Locke Esq.,* 1751, London.
The later image engraved by J. Smith in 1721 exhibits the distinctive upward curl of hair at the neck seen in the 'basso relief'.
John Milton, this is based on the original line engraving by William Faithorne, 1670. A host of secondary copies proliferated and were used on the frontispieces of Milton's published volumes. litt: D. Piper, *Catalogue of 17th century Portraits in the National Portrait Gallery 1625-1714,* 1963, Cambridge Press.
Alexander Pope, it is probable that L.F. Roubiliac's Terra-Cotta bust of Pope modelled in c.1740 and copied many times in marble and other media, is the basis for this image. litt: W. Wimsatt, *The Portraits of Alexander Pope,* New Haven & London, 1965, pp. 223-55.

15. G. Beard, *Italian Stuccoists in Yorkshire,* 1986, York Civic Trust, describes Stucco as a mixture of gypsum (Plaster of Paris) or calcium sulphate, gritty sand, water and powdered marble dust (which is limestone in a crystalline state). It is a mixture capable of fine modelling but usually needs to be built up on wooden or metal armatures. Plaster has a similar mix, but with the addition of animal hair to give it the tensile strength needed.

16. Isaac Ware, *A Complete Body of Architecture,* London, 1756. Ware was most critical of the French manner of the Rococo where 'a ceiling stragled over with arched lines, and twisted curves, with X's and C's and tangled semicircles, may please the light eye of the French, who seldom carry their observation further than a casual glance; but this alone is poor, fantastical, and awkward: Instead of this unmeaning ornament, barely and nakedly scattered over the surface, let our student consider first a graceful outline; next a compartment; each of which may be formed of these kind of figures, softened by his better taste: and let him then find ornaments to intermix with them, to break the familiarity of these figures, and to detain the eye that would be at once perplexed and wearied in following their images'.

17. Cesare Ripa, *Iconologia,* Venice, 1645. A translation of these personifications was provided by George Richardson, *Iconology, or a Collection of Emblematical Figures . . . .,* London, 1779, 2 Vols. He states that 'Abundance is reprefented by the figure of a graceful woman, crowned with a garland of flowers, and dreffed in green robes embroidered with gold. She holds a cornucopia full of fruit and flowers in one hand, in the other a bunch of corn, feveral ears of which are fcattered on the ground. She is reprefented of a graceful afpect, and crowned with flowers, to denote the pleafure and joy we receive from viewing a plentiful harveft. The green robes embroidered with gold, allude to the verdure of the fields, and ripening of the grain. The cornucopia in one hand, and bunch of corn in the other, with the ears fcattered on the ground, are the emblems of Plenty and Abundance.'

18. Sir Roger L. Estrage, *Aesops Fables,* 3rd Edn,1669, Fab.8.
   'A Wolf and a Crane.'
'A Wolf had got a Bone in's Throat, and could think of no better Inftrument to Eafe him of it, than the Bill of a Crane; fo he went and Treated with a Crane to help him out with it, upon Condition of a very considerable Reward for his pains. The Crane did him the Good Office, and then claim'd his Promife. Why how now Impudence: (fays t'other) Do you put your Head into the Mouth of a Wolf, and then. when y'ave brought it out again fafe and found, do you talk of a Reward? Why Sirrah, you have your Head again, and is not that a Sufficient Recompence.'
   'The Moral.'
'One Good Turn they fay requires another: But yet He that has to do with Wild Beafts (as fome Men are No Better) and comes off with a Whol Skin, let him Expect No Other Reward.'

19. The letters of Laurence Sterne, No.176, Jan. 6, 1767, p.292.

20. ZDV(F) F. D.1-21. A typical order placed at the beginning of the winter season with Bartholomew Lawson was for A pipe of Madeira (104 galls), A pipe of Lisbon, A hogshead of Red Port (52 galls), 5 Doz of Old Hock, 4 galls of Canary, 7 bottles of Frontiniac and 115 Doz of Corks and Cappings.
This basic stock would be supplemented at regular intervals with supplies of Old Champagne, Burgundy, Hermitage, Musell (sic) Malmesby and Rivesalt and for more general consumption there were large quantities of Ale, Table beer and small beer laid up in readiness. The average daily consumption of the Fairfax household is estimated at 42 pints of Ale & beer plus 1 bottle of Port and 2 bottles of Sherry a day and the addition of some extra wine on 2/3 days per week.

21. ZDV(F) F.H. 50-83.

22. ZDV(F) F.G. 1-4. John Telford's Supplies for the garden at Gilling and in York show a surprising variety of seeds for the growing of vegetables and herbs. Five different varieties of beans, four types of lettuce, and six of cabbage are amongst the 36 varieties of vegetables planted in the kitchen garden. The herbs are more traditional with such favourites as Endive (chicory), Thyme, Marjoram and Caraway seeds.

23. F. Massiolot, *The Court & Country Cook*, London, 1702. Plan of a dessert table and C. Carter, *The complete Practical Cook*, 1730, p.41. The Dessert thus . . . . . . These illustrations show tall glass stands with long stems and 6-8 glass dishes on which are piled a variety of jellies and sweetmeats. Other supplementary dishes are filled with Portugal Eggs, Almond creams, Plums compote, Barley cream etc. The whole arrangement is both lavish and spectacular. (Information kindly supplied by Peter Brears).

24. C. Gilbert, *The Life & Works of Thomas Chippendale*, 1978, p.46.

25. ZDV(F) L.47, William Grant was paid . . . . . 'for days work making moulds for the ironwork in best staircase . . . . attending Tobin in best staircase . . . .' These balustrades have many similarities with those on the main staircase at Aske Hall.

26. Arthur Stratton, *The English Interior*, 1927. Also illustrates the staircase pl.XCVIII and upper & lower parts of staircase pl. XCIX.

27. George Richardson, fig.136, 'Architettura Militare'.
'This fubject is allegorically reprefented by the figure of a matron, dreffed in a noble garment of divers colours, to denote the various inventions of military conftructions, and its univerfal ufefulnefs. She has a golden chain about her neck, to which is hanging a large diamond, to fignify durability and excellence; this attribute alfo implies that the art of fortification is precious to the ftate, and defends it from the enemy; for this reafon, it is accounted not only an art but a fcience. She is holding the mariners compafs, divided into 360 degrees, and a chart, on which is deciphered the plan of a fortification. A fwallow is flying in the air, which is a bird remarkable for the artificial building of her neft, and is the hieroglyphick of the knowledge of places and fituations for conftructing fortreffes. The pick ax and the fpade lie by the figure, they being the inftruments that are firft neceffary for the erecting of edifices, civil or military.'

28. R.C.H.M. This distinctive motif is to be found at Bransby Hall, Newburgh Priory, Elemore Hall, C.Durham and also in the attributed work at Sutton Park in North Yorkshire.

29. ZDV(F) FN 1-27 These may well be the columns referred to in a series of letters between Fairfax and his London banker Mr. Wright who was unwillingly involved in the transportation by wagon of 'the stones' from London to York.

30. ZDV(F) L.33, 'As the wall opposite the Great Staircase window looks disagreeable I think it would be the cheapest and neatest to run a coat of stucco up and plant flowering shrubs against the low part of it, but this I want your Lordship approbation of before I give orders about it . . . . .'

31. O.N. Wilkinson, *Old Glass*, 1968, pp.147-154. The most common devices seen on Jacobite glasses include the Rose, with two pairs of closed rose buds used to symbolise the young pretender Charles and his brother Henry. Other emblems include the thistle, star, oak leaf, blackbird, wild goose, compass, grub and the butterfly.
The crown modelled on the pennant in the west coving of the great staircase is based on an engraving of the St. Edward's Crown taken from Sandford's, *Coronation of King James II*, 1685. It is perhaps no co-incidence that the Viscount chose an image associated with the last catholic King of England especially when engravings of both the crowns used by George 1st and 2nd were readily available.

32. ZDV(F) L.17, L.62.

33. ZDV(F).

34. Musgrave MS 6991, 257Y, British Museum, *Painted Portraits in Newburgh = ho, Earl Fauconberg*, 1798.

35. ZDV(F) MT.6.

36. ZDV(F) MT.1.

37. *The Temple Newsam Document Collection*, Zoffany Ltd, 27A Motcomb St., Belgrave Sq., London SW1X 8JN. 01-235-5295.

38. ZDV(F) G.1. In 1759 John Telford had supplied 1 blush belgick rose, 3 red belgick roses, 2 blush hundred leav'd roses, a blush provence, a moss provence, 2 marbled and 51 assorted roses for the garden at Gilling.

39. ZDV(F) C.4.

40. Richardson, ...
'Friendship
Is defined the ftate of minds united by perfonal benevolence and intimacy. It is allegorically expreffed by the figure of a woman fimply dreffed in white robes with flowing locks, and crowned with a garland of myrtle and pomegranates. Her breaft is uncovered, and her feet are bare; fhe points to her

heart, and embraces a dry elm tree, entwined with vine branches. The motto longe et prope, (far and near, or alternatively Absent or Present) on the collar about her neck, and that on the hem of her garment, mors et vita, (death and life) fignify that true friendfhip fubfifts, whether the perfon beloved be prefent or abfent, and that it endures for ever. The fimple drefs, the white robes, and flowing locks, indicate, that true Friendfhip is natural, and an enemy to fiction or flattery. The garland of myrtle and flowers of pomegranate, with which the crown is formed, are the fymbols of Love and Concord.

The action of pointing . . . to her heart, denotes fincerity; and her uncovered breaft and bare feet, fignify the readinefs of a friendly mind in ferving others, tho' attended with inconveniences. The dry elm and the vine entwined together, are expreffive of Union, Friendfhip and reciprocal Love, and fignify that a true friend is the fame in adverfity, as in the bloom of profperity'.

The Viscount has introduced minor variations into this scheme with the addition of another motto, Hiems Aestas (Winter or Summer) on a ribbon in the tree. The heart is also mounted on a ribbon held in her right hand and in addition, curious growths sprout from the landscape.

41. Geoffrey Beard, *Italian Stuccoists in Yorkshire*, 1986, pp.14-24.
42. Gainsborough Silks, Sudbury, Suffolk. Bile Green patt. No.792/8910.
43. The Roussillon Gazette, *Journal of the Royal Sussex Regt.* 1933, Vol.20, No.2, Notes on Gen. Charles James Otway. I am grateful to Major J.O. DeSalis for drawing this to my attention.
44. Mixed in with the narcissi, lilies, clematis, poppy, geraniums and primulas are some interesting species of Alpine plants such as the Eritrichium Nanum (King of the Alps), Gentiana Verna, Campanula, Crocus and Saxifragas. Roses also feature in all the arrangements and represent most of the early varieties like R.Gallica, R.Centifolia (the Provence rose), R.Damascena and the more traditional R.Moschata. The more unusual varieties however, are illustrated in the Dining room ceiling and include a Dodicatheon (or shooting star) with its reverse petals and elongated stem and what in the same basket seems to be a Chrysanthemum, despite the fact that apparently the first of these flowers was not introduced into England until 1796. G. Smith, *World of Flowers*, 1988, p.118.
45. Carving by Dick Reid and his workshop. Martin Dutton - 2 pulvinated friezes in Drawing Room and Saloon. Andrew Martindale - mouldings on architrave and Saloon skirting. Kate Thompson - flowers. Gilbert Foucaud - Fretwork on Drawing room dado. Andrew Martindale/Fabiere Egeton - Skirting in Drawing room. Charles Gurney - Oculus stonework. Fabiere Egeton, Kate Thompson and Dick Reid - Palm leaves on Oculus. Six panelled mahogany doors - Hare & Ransome.

46. ZDV(F) MT.4.
The Right Honble Lord Viscount Fairfax
16 Feb. . . . Mary Reynoldson Uphr. Dr. 1766

	£	s	d
For 275yds of Sky & Mixt Damask used for the Hangings of the Drawing Room, 3 pair Window Curtins 8 small and 2 Armed Chairs and one Large Soffa att 7/-yd	96	5	0
152yds of Gold Burnished Border att 6/-yd	45	12	0
70yds Tamy to line Window Curtins, Backs of Chairs and Soffa att 16d yd	4	13	4
8 dozen 2yds Covered Binding used for Curtins 3/-doz.	1	4	6
3 Laths with Pulleys and Brackets used	0	12	0
Rings Tape Silk Thread, Leads used for Window Curtins	1	15	0
For 80ounces of Fringe used for Window Curtins att 2/4d ounce	9	6	8
6 dozen Mixt Line and 12 Tassils and 4 Cloak Pins	1	18	6
Buckeram for the Heads and 84 Brass Hooks	0	5	6
For making up 3 pair Drapery Window Curtins, Tacks and Fixing up the same	2	14	0
8 Mahogone Chairs Fluted Feet Stufft Backs and Seats, To Fine Linnen, Bordering and Wellting the Damask Covers, Gilt Nails Tacks Fringe and Finishing Ditto att 36/- Chair	14	8	0
2 Mahogone Armed Chairs upon Casters Stufft to Fine Linen. Backs Seats and Armes Stufft and *Covered bordering?* and Wellting the Damask Covers, Gilt Nails Fringe Tacks and Finishing Ditto	7	0	0
For Silk and Twist used for the Chairs and Soffa	0	8	0
For Sowing the Damask for the Hangings of the Room and Silk used	1	15	6
For 6yds of Strong Linnen for . . . the Hangings 15d yd.	0	8	1½
Tin of Twopeny Nails, Tacks, 16 ounces Brass Pins used for Hanging the Drawing Room and Fixing on The Gold Borders	1	9	0
	5	0	0
Worked Tassill and Line for the Bell	0	1	6
44 yds Blew and White Check used for 2 Armed Chairs and 8 small Chairs and Large Soffa att 22d yd.	4	0	8
Thread Tape and Making Cases for all	1	0	6
For Large Soffa Mahoganey Frame Upon Casters Carved Scroles & Stufft to Fine Linnen Welting and Bordering The Damask Gilt Nails Frings Tacks and Finishing ditto	14	14	0
	214	11	9½
2 Glasses & Gold and Burnished Frames when filld with Silverd Glass round the Frame	43	10	0

47. H.M. Colvin, *A Biographical Dictionary of English Architects 1660-1840,* p.189.
48. M. Binney, *Constable Burton,* Country Life, Nov.28, 1968.
49. G. Beard, *Italian Stuccoists in Yorkshire,* 1986, York Civic Trust.
50. H.A. Tipping, English Homes, *Tabley House,* 1927, p.27.
51. ZDV(F) L.65.

The Right Honourable Lord Viscount Fairfax Dr
To Maurice Tobin
1762
Aug.st 28th

To 1428 1/2 lb of Iron Work in the Iron railings with Circular Darts top & Bottom of the Pallasadoes at 6 1/2p lb	38 13 9	
To 8 Large ornaments & Iron Bannisters at the Centers & Corners of the Ballustrades at £2.6p lb	18 8 0	
To a hundred double Roses all the Gothick Circular Tops upon the pallasadoes	14 9 0	
To a Curious double Iron Gate in the Center with Diamond pannels Husks & Roses & setting up all the work &c The Lock &c	31 10 0	
	£103 0 9	

Octor: 16th: 1762
Received of the Right Hon.ble Ld Fairfax this Bill in full by me... Maurice Tobin

52. C. Gilbert, *The Life & Work of Thomas Chippendale,* 1978, p.206.
53. Royal Commission on Historic Monuments, *City of York,* Vol.5, p.114.
54. Borthwick Institute: Poor Assessment, St.Mary Castlegate Parish 1744-1789. (PR.Y/MC 103-105).
55. Borthwick Institute: Will of Thomas Barker of Castlegate, York, 1724. He was buried in St.Mary Castlegate church and left his Castlegate property to his nephew Edmund Laycon of Otley, and after his decease, to Edmund's second son Thomas, who in pursuance of his uncle's will, took the name of Barker.
56. The Field, July 1987. Country Life, July 1988.
57. C.R. Markham, *Life of the Great Lord Fairfax,* 1870.
58. C.R. Markham and J.W. Clay, *Genealogies of the Fairfaxes,* c.1870. In addition to the 3 main branches of the family, the main subsidiary branches include the Fairfaxes of the Midland Counties stemming from Hugo Fairfax of Walton, who had manors in Lincolnshire and Nottinghamshire in the 14th century. The Fairfaxes of Australia originated from two members of the Midland Counties branch who settled there in the 19th century.
59. Views of York:
from S.S.E. by Francis Place, 1676.
from S.E. by E.B., 1718.
Buckingham House can be seen in these and other old views of York. Two much smaller houses in a similar 'Dutch' style still exist in the city. One is a rather over-restored house in Ogleforth, but the best remaining house in the post-Restoration style with shaped gables and unusual rusticated brickwork is No.66 Clifton.
60. C.R. Markham, *Life of Admiral Robert Fairfax,* 1885.
61. Fr. Hugh Aveling, *Catholic Recusancy in the City of York, 1967.*
62. Fr. Hugh Aveling, *The Catholic Recusancy of the Yorkshire Fairfaxes:* (Recusant History, article in 3 parts in Vols. 3, 4 and 6, 1955-1961).
63. ZDV (F).
64. *The Journeys of Celia Fiennes 1682-c.1712,* edited by C.Morris, *1982.*
65. *Thomas Baskerville's Journeys in England,* Temp.Car.II: MS Duke of Portland, Welbeck Abbey.
66. John Stevens, *Knavesmire: York's Great Racecourse and its Stories,* 1985.
67. Stewart Lack, *Vavasour Pedigree,* York City Library (Y.929.2).
68. E. Hailstone, *Yorkshire Worthies,* 1868.
69. York City Library, *Yorkshire Pedigrees.*
70. Y.A.J., *Registers of St.Mary's Church, Castlegate,* Vol.15.
71. York City Library, York Directories from 1781.
72. York City Archives, Deeds 25-27 Castlegate, 1919.
73. V.C.H. *A History of York,* 1961, p.417.
74. York Georgian Society, misc. correspondence, 1940-1947.
75. Peter Brown, *The Noel Terry Collection of Furniture and Clocks,* 1987, York Civic Trust.
76. Charles Cator, *A Purely Private Enthusiasm,* Country Life, Sept. 5, 1985.

The York Civic Trust would like to thank the following for permission to reproduce the illustrations:
Church Commissioners: 73, Country Life: Front Cover, 4b, 23, 24a, 31, 36b, 43b, c, 44b, c, 45a, b, 46b, 49, 53a, 55, 74a, b, c, 75, Courtauld Institute of Art: 78a, Evelyn Collection: 10a, 41a, 80, Ferens Art Gallery: Hull City Museums and Art Galleries: 76, Harrogate Museums and Art Galleries: 70, Henry E. Huntington Library and Art Gallery: 72, Institute of Advanced Architectural Studies, York: 43a, R.C.H.M: 46a, c, Dick Reid: 38a, Scottish National Portrait Gallery: 78b, John Shannon: 21a, 22, 28, 34, 39a, b, Sir George Wombwell: 69, Sothebys: 65, Warburg Institute: 25a, 30, York City Art Gallery: 9, 47b, 48a, 68, York City Council: 38b, York City Library: 79. York Civic Trust: all other photographs; colour by Jim Kershaw, Black and White by David Whiteley.